The Instant Cricket Library

AN IMAGINED ANTHOLOGY

The Slattery Media Group Pty Ltd

Level 39/385 Bourke Street, Melbourne

Victoria, Australia, 3000

Text © Dan Liebke, 2018

Design © The Slattery Media Group Pty Ltd, 2018

Published by The Slattery Media Group, 2018

All rights reserved. No part of this publication may be reproduced, stored in a retrieval system or transmitted in any form or by any means without the prior written permission of the copyright owner. Inquiries should be made to the publisher. Inquiries should be made to the publisher.

The Instant Cricket Library is a satirical work.

Cover illustrations: Barry Patenaude

A catalogue record for this book is available from the National Library of Australia

Group Publisher: Geoff Slattery
Editor: Russell Jackson
General and project manager: Jeffrey Sickert
Art Director, Cover Design and Typeset: Kate Slattery
Illustrations: Barry Patenaude

Printed in Australia by Griffin Press

slatterymedia.com

The Instant Cricket Library
AN IMAGINED ANTHOLOGY

DAN LIEBKE

ILLUSTRATIONS BY BARRY PATENAUDE

slattery
MEDIAGROUP

visit *slatterymedia.com*

The Instant Cricket Library

Contents

INTRODUCTION *Rising from the ashes of books about the Ashes* 6

Wicket 9
The Little Master 12
Did Aliens Invent Cricket? 15
The Importance of Being Mitch Marsh 19
The Curious Case of the Cricketer and the Cursed Castle 23
The Future of The Ashes 28
The Loophole 31
Food Theory 35
Struck Down by a Queer Spell 39
An Amazing Day Off 43
The Rise of Speed 47
The Battle of Eden 51

It's The End of the World Cup as We Know It 56
A Tiny Ripple of Hope 60
The Sights and the Sounds 63
The Stunning Secret Origin of Banner-Man! 66
Introduction to International Cricket: a Timeline 68
Christmas Comes Early 73
Listomania 77
Cricket Goes Deluxe 82
Masking the Darkness 87
Head in the Clouds 90
Infinite Improbability Drive 93
Popular Landmarks for the Ashes Holiday Bucket List 97

AN IMAGINED ANTHOLOGY

The Truth Behind Allegations of Spot-Fixing-Fixing	101	Waiting For a Return	145
Wicked Maidens	105	Astonishing True Secret No.41 - Murali's Mural	151
Freeway of Finality	109	Meeting Minutes: Third Ashes Test, 2017-18	155
Averages, Geometry and Combinatorics - the Quiz	113	'The Battles of Dawson'	159
The Modern Game	117	The Art of Warner	163
Jedis, Jokers & The Don	121	The Genius of Bad Cricket	166
Being The Best	123	'What I Learned About Mateship Down Under'	170
Handled The Ball	126	Bulging Lists and Unsolicited Tips	172
Expanded Cricket Roles	131	The Perimeter of Identity	178
Calling It In	135	The Book of Botham 19:81	181
A Serpent's Lament	139		

'Author' biographies 185

INTRODUCTION

Rising from the ashes of books about the Ashes

I n the following pages you'll find excerpts from a number of cricket books, none of which you've ever read before. There's *I, Pad,* Shane Watson's infamous manifesto arguing that the LBW Law should be abolished. There's *Out of My Ed,* in which we discover the truth about the *real* Ed Cowan. There's a Banner-Man comic book, a Mitch Marsh play, and much more.

They're all part of the Instant Cricket Library.

Imagine a world after a complete societal collapse. A big collapse, like Australia on a raging Chennai turner. In this dystopian future, all of the world's cricket books have been destroyed.

Nothing remains, not even the Steve Waugh autobiographies, which were previously believed to be impervious not just to casual readers, but to all known forms of physical damage.

And yet, a hardy group of researchers search desperately for hints of what might have been lost. A title here. A snippet of text there. A tattered cover somewhere else. They gather these fragments of information.

The researchers talk to the elders—those who remember the time before 'The Collapse'. They piece together more details from their fading and addled memories. They gather every piece of knowledge they've found, all the clues they've discovered of the lost world of cricketing literature, and enter them into a hastily constructed supercomputer.

Finally, with a burst of makeshift artificial intelligence, they extrapolate from those fragments and regenerate a complete cricket library in an instant.

This instant cricket library is a marvel of resourcefulness, and a glorious tribute to the ingenuity and determination of humanity, even when faced with the most nightmarish and cricketless of futures.

Which is why it's such a shame that the researchers got it so completely wrong.

None of the books in this anthology existed. Shane Watson did not write an anti-LBW manifesto. One can only guess the true nature of Ed Cowan's character. There was never a comic book called Banner-Man, nor a play about Mitch Marsh.

But if there had been, this is what they might have looked like. So read on. Just because a cricket book never existed doesn't mean it's not worth reading.

Dan Liebke,
August 2018

*All the content in this book
is imagined, although the names
may not be.*

*The author has a vivid imagination,
a passable knowledge of the history
of cricket and its characters,
and an unfortunate fondness
for the art of satire*

Wicket

**AN EXCERPT FROM THE ENCYCLOPAEDIA
OF ALL CRICKETING KNOWLEDGE**

*Sometimes cricket terminology can be confusing.
But this handy guide should get beginners up to speed.*

A **wicket** is a set of **stumps** and **bails** that is placed at either end of a **pitch**, or **wicket**. If the **wicket** is struck by the ball, then the batsman loses their **wicket**, providing the **bails** are broken and the ball is not a **no ball**.

(Balls that are **no balls** are not considered balls, in accordance with the logical axiom of negation.)

The **bails** may be broken by a non-**no ball** striking the **stumps** directly. In this case, the bowler has **bowled** the batsman.

Alternatively, a breaking of the **bails** may cost the batsman their **wicket** if the batsman is **stumped** by being too far down the **wicket** (either because they **bail** out of their shot or are **stumped** by the flight of the ball). However, the batsman keeps their **wicket** if the **wicket** keeper fails to **stump** the batsman despite their being down the **wicket**.

It should be noted that **stumpings** after **stumps** do not count, and the batsman does not lose their **wicket** even if their **wicket** would otherwise have been taken. **Wickets** cannot fall after **stumps** in much the same way that **wickets** cannot fall off **no balls**. Except, of course, for those **wickets** that can.

If a ball is a **no ball** then the batsman's **wicket** may still fall if the **stumps** are broken (prior to **stumps**) and the batsman is **run out**.

(Batsmen who **run out** when their **bail** has been broken may be pursued by a bounty hunter, in accordance with the legal axiom of **bail recovery**.)

Even when **no ball** strikes the **wicket**, a **wicket** may still fall, although again not if the ball is a **no ball**. A batsman may be **leg before wicket**, for example.

A batsman is **leg before wicket** if the umpire judges the ball would have struck the **stumps** and **bowled** the batsman had it not hit the batsman's **leg**. The umpire will assess where the ball **pitched** in making his judgment. **No ball** that **pitches** outside **leg stump** should be given **leg before wicket**, especially if it is a **no ball**. However, batsmen do still sometimes lose their **wicket** this way, due to faulty judgement on where the ball **pitched** or the failure to spot a **no ball**. It can be difficult for an umpire to watch the **leg** of the bowler for a **no ball** and also keep an eye on the other end of the **pitch**.

If the batsman is struck outside the **off stump** they may also still be **leg before wicket** if the umpire judges them to have played no shot to the ball. (Playing no shot to a ball is different from playing a shot to a **no ball**.) The umpire must still judge whether the ball would have struck the **stumps** and **bowled** the batsman, had the batsman's **leg** not prevented it.

A batsman may be out **leg before wicket** even if the ball strikes some part of their body other than their **leg** and the umpire judges that the batsman would have otherwise been **bowled**. In such a case, the **wicket** will still be designated **leg before wicket** even though neither the **leg** nor the **wicket** was involved. The usual **leg before wicket** conditions for where the ball **pitches** and whether the ball is a **no ball** shall apply.

As tempting as it might be, the umpire cannot claim to be **stumped** as to where the ball **pitched**. The umpire must make a decision. However, the umpire *may* confess to being **stumped** by whether the ball is a **no ball** and ask for a **review** of where the bowler's **leg** landed. The batsman may also ask for a **review** of a **leg before wicket** decision. The **review** will consider if the ball was a **no ball**, along with where the ball **pitched** and whether the ball would have hit the **stumps**.

A batsman may not **review** if there are no **reviews** remaining. A batsman may have no **reviews** remaining because previous decisions to **review** had been **off**, and, as a result, the **wicket** had not been overturned.

Batsmen rarely **review** decisions where **wickets** are overturned. **Stumps** being turned over and over by the ball are almost always out, **bowled**. Unless, of course, the ball is a **no ball**. But **reviewing** a **no ball** is considered an act of desperation. Although not if the **review** of the **no ball** is made by the umpire.

A batsman may also be **caught**.

(If a batsman is **caught** by a bounty hunter employed by a **bail** bondsman, they will go before a judge and make their **pitch** to be let **off**. This is, admittedly, rare.)

It really is that simple.

The Little Master

THE INTRODUCTION TO 'JESSIE, COME AND HAVE A LOOK AT THIS YOUNG MAN' BY LADY JESSIE BRADMAN

Lady Jessie Bradman stunned the cricketing world when she released her memoir of life with The Don, which was full of insightful breakdowns of some of the finest cricketers of the 1990s.

"Jessie, come and have a look at this young man," he would call from the lounge room.

Invariably, dear reader, I would then sigh heavily, swear beneath my breath, put to one side whatever more important task I was attempting to complete, and dutifully wander in to look at whoever it was the old boy had spotted on television this time.

He'd only started behaving this way when we'd got our first widescreen TV. Don had been so excited as it was installed, barking orders at the burly, muscular man from Harvey Norman as he attached it to the wall and tuned the various channels.

Don had most definitely not urged me to come in and look at *that* young man. But I'd done so anyway, glancing surreptitiously in from the kitchen while I prepared some morning tea.

"Which channel has the cricket?" Don demanded, even before the handsome man had finished.

The man tried to explain that it depended on whether it was a home series broadcast on free-to-air TV or an overseas series shown only on Pay-TV. He gave Don the various remote controls and showed him how to change the input source on the television and which device would then control the volume, but Don was of no mind to listen.

"This is all too hard," he complained, so the next day I ordered him a universal remote control. I then programmed it so he could always find the cricket with the press of a single button.

Yeah, Jessie. *Brilliant* move. Real smart. For as soon as Don had control of the television with its rich colours, deep blacks, ultra-sharp images and never-ending access to televised cricket, the terrible phrase began to emerge from his lips.

"Jessie, come and have a look at this young man."

Inevitably, once I made my way to the lounge room, Don would point at the television screen and ask me if the person on it reminded me of him. They never did, of course. The crazy old codger.

One time, it was Mark Taylor, who I was quick to point out was a somewhat dour and limited left-handed accumulator of runs, very different in style from Don's right-handed flashing blade. He didn't listen, instead claiming over and over that Taylor would someday match his record score of 334. I was sceptical, but I knew that even if he did, he sure as blazes wouldn't be scoring most of those runs in a single day. It wasn't 'how many' that I was disputing, it was 'how'.

Another time it was Jonty Rhodes, who, bless his heart, bore no resemblance to my doddery husband at any point in his life. I think Don was just fond of his relentlessly upbeat attitude. "He's so full of pluck," he would say. "Remember the time he jumped into the stumps?" And I would have to nod and say that I did, indeed, remember that time. Because what the actual heck else was I going to say? Don would then cackle merrily away at the memory, before asking me if I remembered the time *he* jumped into the stumps. And I would have to tell him that never happened.

Brian Lara, Alec Stewart, Steve Waugh, Mike Atherton, Aravinda de Silva, Gary Kirsten, Inzamam-ul-Haq, Carl Hooper, David Boon, Stephen Fleming. All of them merited at one time or another the dread cry of "Jessie, come and have a look at this young man", before I had to patiently explain how their batting style differed substantially from his own.

On one occasion he telephoned me at a CWA jazzercise class to come look at Wasim Akram's bowling action, which he suddenly declared to be very similar to his own. I didn't even know where to begin with that one. Eventually I had to patiently break down all the differences between the Pakistan left-arm champion's in-swinging yorkers and Don's gentle right arm leg spin. I'm still not sure I convinced him.

It never got any better. One time during the 1996 Olympics he declared Linford Christie's running style to be similar to his own. Then there was the time he questioned if Chandler's quick wit on the television show *Friends* reminded me of him. Or the time while watching an old episode of *Doctor Who* when he wondered aloud if The Doctor might have been able to bounce golf balls off Daleks using just a cricket stump.

Utter. Flipping. Madness. Eventually, of course, I broke. One day, he summoned me in to look at Sachin Tendulkar and, finally fed up, I told him that sure, Tendulkar reminded me of him. Why not? The Little Master was close enough. More importantly, it was the only way I was ever going to get any respite from Don's ceaseless determination to find his modern-day counterpart.

All of this is my way of introducing the genesis of this book. I'm going to spend a few hundred pages chronicling all the young men who Don urged me to come and have a look at, from Arjuna Ranatunga all the way through to Sachin Tendulkar, via Navjot Sidhu, Ken Rutherford, that macaw he saw once on an Attenborough special, and all the rest.

Let's get cracking, shall we?

Did Aliens Invent Cricket?

**AN EXCERPT FROM 'CHERRIES OF THE GODS',
SELF-PUBLISHED BY SHANE WARNE**

*The master spinner's belief in aliens peaked with
the release of his 'alienifesto', explaining
the extra-terrestrial origins of cricket*

Before we move on to talk about Atlantis, UFOs and Marlen [sic] Samuels, we need to sort out, once and for all, if aliens invented cricket.

I reckon they did. Historians say that cricket evolved from other bat and ball sports, but think about it—if they did, then why aren't those other bat and ball sports still around? It doesn't make sense. I think aliens came down and said 'let's have a bit of this' and bang! Cricket.

People say, 'What about baseball?'. But baseball's pretty much the same as softball and T-ball and rounders and stuff like that. They're the kind of sports a human would invent. Cricket's a lot different.

It's like the pyramids. Humans couldn't make the pyramids. You couldn't pull those ropes, huge bits of brick and make it perfectly

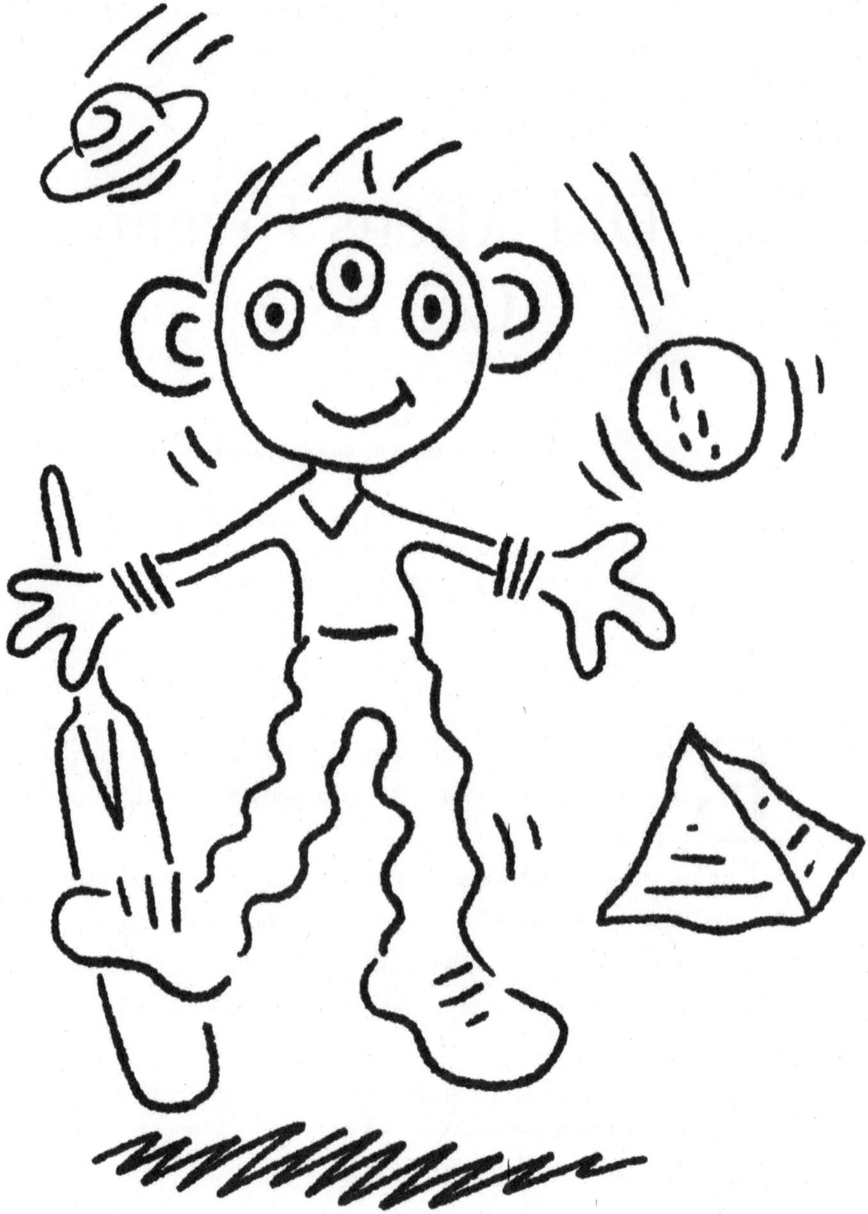

symmetrical. Couldn't do it. So who did it?

Cricket's the same as the pyramids. Could a human think of all those umpire's gestures? The LBW law? Mankads? No. So who did? I'm saying aliens.

Here's something. You know how a pitch is precisely 22 yards long? Well, I've heard that 22 is the atomic number for Titanium. And Titan is one of Saturn's moons, which is supposably one of the only other places in the Solar system that can support life.

Did the aliens from Titan come down to Earth and invent cricket? I don't know for sure. But I *am* saying I don't think we can rule it out. To the left I've included a drawing of what I reckon the aliens looked like.

Why does cricket take so long to play? Maybe the Titanians have different life spans than us. Maybe five days for them is like the length of a footy game for us. Like when Matthew McConaughey's time got messed up going down to that wave planet in *Interstellar*. Don't ask me how that works, by the way. Those sci-fi movies do my head in, and I'm adding *Interstellar* to my list of things that are overrated, along with queuing, holding hands and that slice of lemon they put in your glass of water at fancy restaurants. As for movies, give me *American Pie* any day; it's funny but still pretty smart in its own way too, without being bigheaded about it. Seriously, how good is Stifler! He just cracks me up. Such a knob, but you can't not laugh.

But the longer alien lifespan makes sense, when you think about it. That's also why the aliens never needed super-slo-mo to detect close run outs. They had more time to see if a batsman made his ground. Why do we bowl with straight arms (no offence, Murali!!)? I reckon it's because the aliens don't have elbows. But that means when they take a tea break, or are thirsty for a cold one after stumps, they need to use straws. But here's the thing: drinking straws weren't patented until 1888, but Test cricket began in 1877! If cricket needed technology that humans hadn't even invented yet to be played properly, then yeah, it all comes back to aliens.

What else do we know about the aliens? Well, to help them hear a feather through to the keeper, they've probably got bigger ears than Gilly! Ha ha ha! And maybe they have super-hard skulls and super-soft legs so they didn't need any padding like we do. I bet they'd love smashing a dirty rotten spag bol pizza too. Who doesn't?

Here's the team I reckon we should select to take on the aliens if they ever come back and want to play cricket against us:

Tubs Taylor (c)
Sachin Tendulkar
Ian Chappell
Brian Lara
Michael Clarke
Allan Border
Darren 'Chuck' Berry (wk)
Beefy Botham
Me (ha ha! sorry but I'm playing against the aliens, for sure)
Wasim Akram
Pigeon
Viv Richards (12th man)
Umpire: Billy Bowden
Coach: None! Not needed! The only coach we'll have is the one we'll be driving to the match in. Ha ha ha!

Also, Stonehenge. You can't tell me those rocks don't look like cricket stumps. And we know aliens built Stonehenge, so it all makes sense when you think about it. (By the way, Stonehenge? Way overrated.)

Anyway, that's what I reckon about aliens. Definitely built the pyramids. Definitely invented cricket.

Next: Marlen [sic] Samuels.

The Importance of Being Mitch Marsh

In the opening scene from the long-running play, the stage is set for a farcical series of escalating events.

ACT I
SCENE 1

[AUSTIN, a slick up-and-coming promotions officer at Cricket Australia, is meeting with his father, STEVE, a two-bit toy-maker, in the latter's workshop to discuss the shipment of Mitch Marsh action figures he ordered for the Boxing Day Test]

AUSTIN: Hey dad, CA is on my back about the action figures.

STEVE: (ever so slightly nervously) Sorry to hear that, son.

AUSTIN: No big deal. They just want to know how soon we can get the merch.

STEVE: The merch?

AUSTIN: The Mitch merch.

STEVE: You mean the Marsh merch?

AUSTIN: The Mitch Marsh merch, yes. How soon can I get it?

STEVE: (flipping through a desk diary) Uhh... March.

AUSTIN: March?

STEVE: March.

AUSTIN: (incredulously) The summer will be over by March. Mitch Marsh merch in March is no good to anybody.

STEVE: I'm sorry, but I just can't make much more Mitch Marsh merch. Not until March.

AUSTIN: Dad, I need my Mitch Marsh merch by next match or I'll lose my job.

STEVE: How much Mitch Marsh merch do you need?

AUSTIN: How much Mitch Marsh merch do you have?

STEVE: (sheepishly) Two crates.

AUSTIN: Two crates?

STEVE: I know that's not too great.

AUSTIN: Two crates? What in blazes is taking so long?

STEVE: Torque rates.

AUSTIN: What?

STEVE: The factory's having problems with the Mitch Marsh machinery.

AUSTIN: The Mitch Marsh machinery's torque rates?

STEVE: Yes.

AUSTIN: And because of the Mitch Marsh machinery torque rates you only have two crates of Mitch Marsh merch?

STEVE: Yes.

AUSTIN: (sighing) Maybe we can mooch Mitch Marsh merch from somewhere else?

[AUSTIN looks around the room, his gaze finally resting at an action figure on the bookshelf in the corner]

AUSTIN: (continued) What's on the shelf there?

STEVE: What, son?

AUSTIN: I said, what's on the shelf?

STEVE: Watson.

AUSTIN: (confused, slowly, as if his father is an idiot) Yes. What's on the shelf?

STEVE: (just as confused, just as slowly, as if his son is an idiot) Watson.

AUSTIN: Yes, what's on?

STEVE: No. (He finally picks up the doll and shows it to Austin). It's Shane Watson. See?

AUSTIN: (pondering) Hmmm… Do you have much Shane Watson merch?

STEVE: Crates and crates.

AUSTIN: Great. (He peers at the Watson doll again) Do you think you can make this match Mitch?

STEVE: Match Mitch Marsh?

AUSTIN: Yes.

STEVE: We'd have to get rid of a lot of the hair.

AUSTIN: A shorn Watson.

STEVE: It's Shane Watson.

AUSTIN: Yes. A shorn Shane Watson. To look like Marsh.

STEVE: Shaun Marsh?

AUSTIN: No. Not Shaun Marsh. A shorn Mitch Marsh.

STEVE: Shaun and Mitch Marsh?

AUSTIN: No, just Mitch Marsh.

STEVE: But shorn.

AUSTIN: Yes.

STEVE: But not Shaun.

AUSTIN: No.

STEVE: Sure?

AUSTIN: Very sure.

STEVE: You'd end up with a mishmash of mismatched Mitch Marsh merch.

AUSTIN: A mishmash of mismatched Mitch Marsh merch next match mollifies me much more than matched Mitch Marsh merch next March.

STEVE: That's easy for you to say.

(End scene)

The Curious Case of the Cricketer and the Cursed Castle

BY SIR ARTHUR CONAN MORRIS

The game is afoot in a classic mystery featuring master detective Sherlock Hohns and his sidekick Watson.

It had just gone 2am in late June, '05, when there was a knock on the door. I was still awake, curled on the floor, unable to sleep from the horrors I'd just witnessed. But for the same reason, I was also wary of what the source of the rapping on the door might be.

"Are you in there, Watson?" came a voice from the other side of the door. I recognised it immediately and sprang from the floor.

"Hohns," I said, as I opened the door. "Thank goodness you're here. Please come in."

Hohns did so. He was fully dressed, wide-eyed and alert, with seemingly no ill-effects from being roused at this untimely hour.

"I believe you know Mr Lee," I said, gesturing to the gentleman who'd

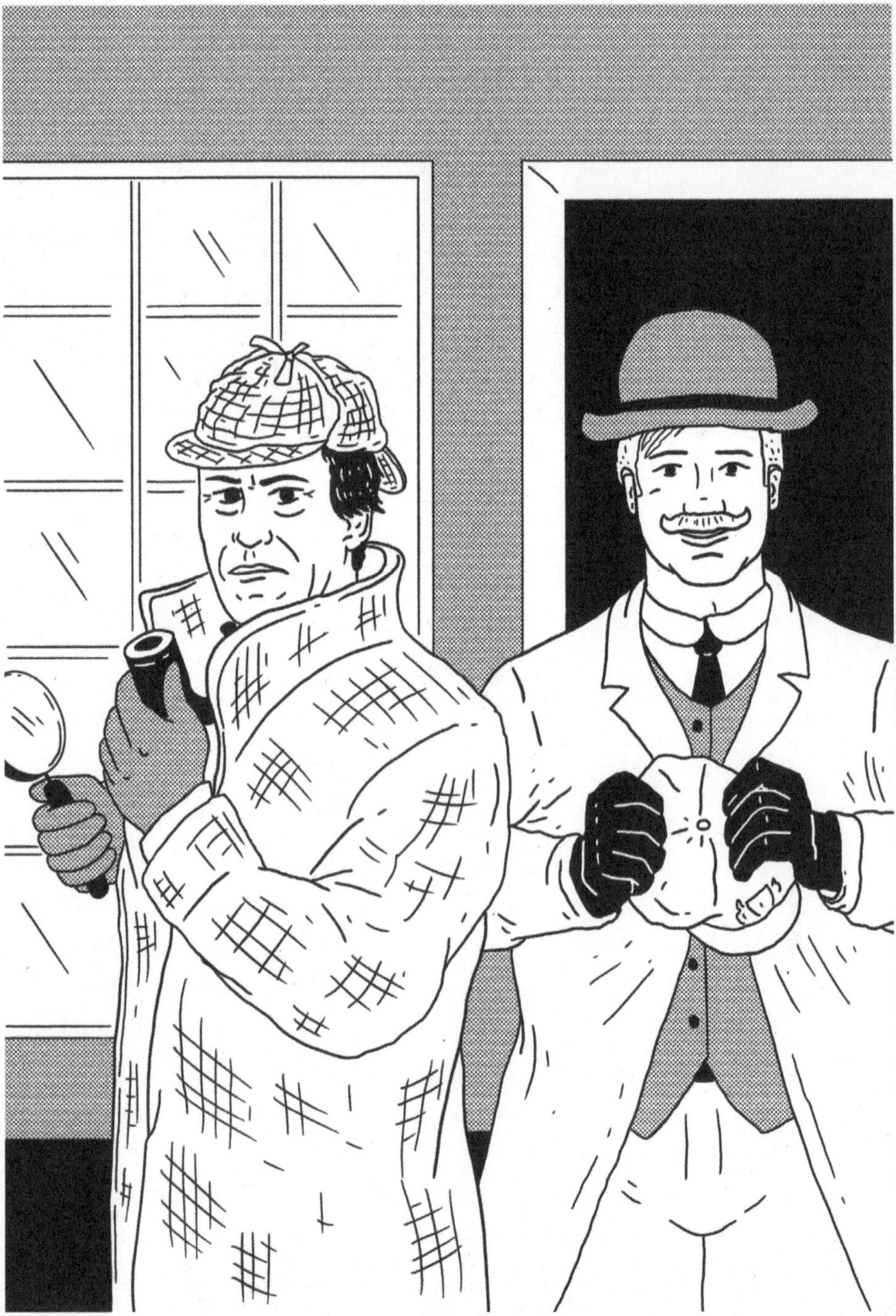

kindly allowed me to stay in his room following the incident. "Mr Lee, this is Sherlock Hohns."

"Brett," nodded Hohns. "I see you've been dreaming about a Tony Abbott prime ministership again."

"How did you know that?" said Mr Lee, swiftly reaching for his dressing gown.

"A trifling deduction," said Hohns, waving the question away. "But that's not why you've called me here, is it? Indeed, I believe you have a ghost story to tell me, Watson."

I had always admired the rapid deductions of Hohns, as swift as intuitions, and yet always founded on a logical basis. As a private selector, he'd investigated many cricketers' careers and some of the conclusions he'd made had been remarkable. And yet, I was still amazed at this feat of inference.

"How could you possibly have known that?" I said.

"Elementary, my dear Watto. The bags under your eyes suggest that you have not slept since the team arrived here at Lumley Castle," began Hohns. "I also note the tear in your Buzz Lightyear pyjamas; a tear that precisely matches the piece of fabric I saw outside the door of your hotel room, as if you'd fled in a hurry. Furthermore, I see that while you were awaiting my arrival, you were reading by torchlight a copy of 'Lily of Lumley—The Ghost That Haunts Lumley Castle'. All of this suggests that you were scared by a ghost and escaped to the safety of Mr Lee's room."

"Astonishing," I said.

"Not at all," said Hohns. "Now, pray tell me what you saw in your room."

"It was a horrifying spectre, Hohns," I said, trying to compose myself. "I was settling in for the evening with a hot mug of Nesquick chocolate milk, thinking about how I could counteract the swing of the Duke ball in English conditions. That's when I heard the moans."

"Moans?" said Hohns.

"Maybe groans," I said.

"Moans or groans," said Hohns. "Any other unknowns?"

"It spoke to me, Hohns," I said. "In a low voice. 'Wattoooo,' it said. 'Waaattttooooo.' And then I saw it."

"What did you see?" asked Hohns.

"Just the outline of the ghost," I said. "In the corner of my room, going through my kit. I couldn't make out its details. All I could see were its eyes. Dark and cold and pitiless. I fled immediately to the safety of Mr Lee's room."

Hohns nodded. "That's an interesting review of the situation, Watson," he said. "But I fear it's a review you've got terribly wrong."

Mr Lee began to giggle at this, but stopped as Hohns shot him a glare.

"May I suggest the following alternative scenario?" said Hohns, lighting up his pipe. "When you first arrived at the castle, your baggy green went missing, did it not?"

"How could you have kn—"

"A yes or no will suffice, Watson," said Hohns.

"Yes," I said.

"But you were able to retrieve it from the Lost and Found, correct?"

I nodded and reached for the headwear, which I'd been using as a makeshift pillow. I handed the cap to Hohns.

"And this is definitely *your* baggy green?" said Hohns.

"Yes," I said. I gestured to the monogram on the inside. "See? 'S.W.' As in Shane Watson."

Hohns nodded. "It's rather tattered, don't you think?" he said. "For a cap you received fewer than six months ago."

"I assume it was treated poorly in the Lost and Found," I said.

"Or," said Hohns. "This cap belongs to another Australian cricketer with initials S.W. A man who checked into the castle just two days ago, according to the guest ledger. A man who lost his famously decrepit baggy green, only to have you take it. Just as you took his spot in the Australian

ODI side prior to the 2003 World Cup."

Mr Lee gasped. "But weren't *you* responsible for Watson taking that spot from him, Hohns?" he said.

Hohns removed the pipe from his mouth and glared again at Mr Lee. "Please do up your dressing gown, sir," he said.

"You mean… the ghost is Steve Waugh?" I said. This was a prospect more terrifying than any undead creature. "But why wouldn't he just *ask* for the cap back?"

"When you've spent a lifetime mentally disintegrating people, it can be a hard habit to break," said Hohns. "Nevertheless, I'm sure if I return the baggy green to Mr Waugh, that shall be the end of the matter."

"Amazing!" I exclaimed. "Hohns, you've done it again."

The Future of The Ashes

AN EXCERPT FROM 'MY AUTOBIOGRAPHY (REVISED EDITION, 2012)' BY KEVIN PIETERSEN

Yet another revision of one of Kevin Pietersen's numerous autobiographies

I'm not as cocky as my image suggests, so after claiming in my 2006 autobiography ('My Autobiography' by Kevin Pietersen) that Shane Warne could *never* bowl me around my legs, you can imagine how I felt when he did just that in the 2006/07 Ashes. I was embarrassed. Humiliated. Humbled.

You can be certain I won't be making mistakes like that[1] in this 2012 autobiography.

But what I can confidently say is that, having retained the Ashes 3-1 in Australia in 2010/11, there's absolutely no reason[2] why we can't hold onto them for more than a decade, like Australia did through the 1990s.

---

1 Dear me. It seems like I did make those mistakes again. Well, you can be sure I won't make those mistakes in my next autobiography.
2 There is one[2a] reason. And that reason is that Australia were simply too good in the 2013/14 Ashes and won them back.
    [2a] Actually, there were a multitude of other reasons for our failure on that tour. See my 2015 autobiography ('My Autobiography' by Kevin Pietersen) for details. In short, the whole tour was a never-ending joke that cost me my international career. But am I bitter about this? No[2aa], no, and no again.
    [2aa] Well, maybe a little.

Our captain Andrew Strauss can lead the team for many more years[3]. The respect[4] he has for me as a player and a man gives me the confidence I need to play at my very, very best. The coaching of Andy Flower is superb[5], but the spirit he builds in the team is even better[6]. Our bowling unit of Jimmy Anderson, Stuart Broad, Steven Finn and Graeme Swann is not just highly talented, but a friendlier[7] bunch of blokes you'll never meet. And don't get me started on Matt Prior, who is simply an absolute gem[8] behind the stumps and in the dressing room.

Who do Australia have? My goodness, their bowlers are unthreatening. I think we all know by now that Mitchell Johnson will never[9] get it right on a consistent basis. Ryan Harris is too injury-prone to play more than one Test at a time[10]. And Peter Siddle is nothing more than a trundler who any international batsman would be embarrassed to be dismissed by[11]. Yes, Michael Beer is a strong spinning prospect for Australia[12] but I firmly believe he can be countered[13]. Steve Smith's lucky half-century in the Fifth Test shouldn't distract him. Yes, you made a Test half-century, young man. Well done. But bank that as something to tell the grandkids one day and move on to working on your leg-spin, where you can support

---

3 He retired six weeks after this autobiography was published
4 He later called me a c*** on television.
5 'superb' was a silly, silly typo. I obviously meant to say 'superbad'.
6 Flower was, in fact, a Mood-Hoover™, who sucked the fun out of everything he came near. (Please note that Mood-Hoover™ is a registered trademark of Kevin Pietersen Entertainment Pty Limited, and has been licensed to the upcoming Netflix cartoon series 'Klever Kevin and the Mood-Hoover Marauders!')
7 Well, Finny's fine.
8 A potato gem. Encased in a big block of cheese.
9 People often tell me I'm a batting genius. And yes, there are times when I'm in the zone that I can see why. But if there was ever a fast-bowling genius, it was Mitchell Johnson during that 2013-14 series. He was hostile, aggressive, unplayable. And weren't our big-talking bowling line-up reduced to pathetic little schoolboys when facing him?
10 He somehow played ten Tests in a row in that period, including nine against England. Absolutely astonishing from a man with no functioning knees. As another champion who also suffered from chronic knee injuries, I know the agony that Ryan Harris must have gone through. All I can say is that he was fortunate to have a team around him that supported his unique circumstances and didn't try to bring him down with petty sniping or parody Twitter accounts.
11 I was dismissed by Peter Siddle more than any other bowler. Am I embarrassed? Of course not. Siddle was a quality bowler and an absolutely champion bloke. Anybody who calls him a trundler simply doesn't know what they're talking about.
12 He wasn't.
13 He was.

Beer in the future[14].

But no matter what Australia do, the fact remains that this is a very special England team—a great team and a great group of friends[15]. I think we'll be together, dominating Australia, for a long, long time[16].

---

14 Or you could be the next best batsman after Bradman. It's up to you, Steve. My goodness, did I read that wrong. Still, live and learn, as my good friend Piers Morgan likes to say.
15 (sigh) Yes, I know.
16 I can't hear you. I can't hear you, mate.

The Loophole

**AN EXCERPT FROM 'THE NEW MONEYBALL—
HOW THE MELBOURNE RENEGADES ALLOWED A NERD
TO TURN T20 FRANCHISE CRICKET ON ITS HEAD'**

*Could the baseball principles of 'Moneyball' achieve similar success
in cricket? One BBL team was determined to find out.*

Bobby Braccoli crunched the numbers over and over again, almost unable to believe the results he was seeing.

Braccoli had been hired by the Melbourne Renegades six months ago. This followed a summer in which the Renegades had finished a startling ninth place in a competition containing only eight teams, thanks to salary cap penalties and a poor net run rate.

Braccoli's mission was to bring the Renegades backroom into the 21st century—to transform it from a franchise built entirely on gut feel and wayward throwdowns to one supported by scientific analysis using cutting-edge sabermetric principles.

Braccoli had never seen a contest of cricket in his life and barely knew the difference between a Cameron White and a Chris Green. (In his primary school years Braccoli had been diagnosed as legally colour blind.) But he was a bona fide mathematical genius with a Ph.D in Probability Theory and Fuzzy Logic.

From Braccoli's perspective, the 240 deliveries that defined a typical T20 match constituted a stochastic[1] system, and he was perfectly capable of analysing it. All he needed was the data. And that was easy enough to illegally torrent and scrape.

His initial analysis immediately generated ideas worth implementing for easy marginal gains.

Marginal gains weren't to be downplayed. Every edge a team could gain, no matter how minor, was cumulative and could mean the difference between victory or defeat.

For example, it was easy enough to prove that the shorter the format of the game, the less predictable the result. T20s were more prone to upsets than ODI matches, which in turn were more prone to upsets than Test matches.

Extrapolating, that implied that a Super Over was more volatile again. So against stronger teams, the correct strategy was to attempt to *tie* the match rather than win it. In doing so, you transformed the match into a one-over game where you had a much better chance of jagging an against-the-odds win.

Aiming for a tie rather than a win meant one fewer run to deal with—not much, but a crucial edge they could take on board against stronger opposition.

Braccoli had put forth this idea to team management, who'd embraced it enthusiastically and encouraged him to drill further into the data. His revolutionary 'tie theory' was but one example.

Now, after a detailed, four-month analysis of the entire history of T20 franchise cricket, he'd found another loophole, one that would change everything. In a way, it seemed almost too simple. But after triple-checking his results, he printed them out and ran down the hall to Andrew McDonald, the team coach.

---

1 A 'stochastic' system is one in which moving from each individual stage to the next is unpredictable, but taken as a whole, certain patterns and trends can be observed. Like, for example, the international career of Shaun Marsh.

"What if I told you that I could improve your team's use of batting resources by a factor of five?" said Braccoli.

McDonald's eyes narrowed. "I'd be sceptical," he said.

Braccoli shoved the printout into his hands. "Don't be," he said. He went on to explain what the printout's myriad tables and graphs showed.

In any given season, Braccoli explained, between 19% and 22% of wickets to fall were clean bowled. This implied that approximately 80% of wickets fell by other means. But a careful examination of the Laws and Playing Conditions of the Big Bash League made it clear that every other form of dismissal was *completely avoidable*.

Caught? Hit the ball along the ground. If never hitting in the air was good enough for the legendary Dan Bradman, supposedly the best BBL player of the 1930s, back before domestic T20 records were kept, it would be good enough for the Renegades.

Leg Before Wicket? Always, always keep your pads outside the line of leg stump and you will never be LBW.

Stumped? Never leave your crease and you won't be stumped.

Run Out? Never run. You can make runs entirely in boundaries. Not sixes, because that requires hitting in the air, but fours are perfectly adequate—and you only need roughly two per over to attain a par score.

All the other dismissals are just as easy to avoid, Braccoli went on to explain. So avoidable they almost never took place anyway.

But by retaining only clean bowled as a possible method of dismissal, players will be suddenly 80% less likely to be dismissed on any given ball, which translates to a batting innings five times longer. This improvement in batting resources would comfortably compensate for any negative impact introduced by the players changing a lifetime of cricketing experience.

McDonald was instantly won over by Braccoli's detailed analysis and enthusiastically implemented his plan. The Renegades scoured world cricket, recruiting the batsmen with the highest proportion of bowled dismissals. For players already in the squad with poor records at being bowled, McDonald spent the winter months working on pushing their batting stance further leg side and never hitting the ball in the air.

As a bonus, McDonald found that by encouraging his batsmen to never run, the non-striker could take a mental break for six balls at a time. This excited the Renegades coach and underpinned most of the considerable investment in mindfulness training for the players during the pre-season. Now the breakthrough approach derived from Braccoli's loophole was also completely changing the mental side of the game.

Renegades by name. Renegades by nature.

And yet, despite a stunning 98.3% of their batsmen being bowled in the following BBL season (Aaron Finch fell onto his stumps in one game while adjusting his new batting stance), the Renegades still finished last on the table. Shockingly, by an even larger margin than in any previous year.

What had gone wrong? Braccoli couldn't put his finger on it. But he was determined to go back to the drawing board and find out.

Food Theory

**AN EXCERPT FROM 'LIVING A JARDINE LIFE:
A GUIDE TO EXPLOITING THE LOOPHOLES OF EVERYDAY LIFE'
BY DOUGLAS JARDINE, COURTESY OF THE DOUGLAS JARDINE ESTATE**

Douglas Jardine's acclaimed self-help book encourages readers to exploit society's loopholes, giving them a head start over those who indulge in social niceties.

Now that you've used my methods from the previous chapter to secure yourself a job, free suit and dashing multi-coloured harlequin cap, it's time to ensure your hard-earned[1] wages don't go to waste.

A lot of people will claim these techniques aren't fair play. But we're not interested in social niceties. The bastards who tell you there's no such thing as a free lunch simply haven't examined the problem from all the angles.

Nor is this a matter of skinflintery. I have neither the intention nor the desire to give grocers, restaurateurs, and cafe owners my money when they have obvious food-selling weaknesses I can exploit. Neither should you. Especially when, with the application of the following simple ploys,

---

1 Of course, you won't be working hard for your money. In the next chapter, I'll show you tips to rise to the top of your career without the tedium of completing any work tasks. Just because somebody is more naturally gifted and hard-working than you, that's no reason to let them get ahead.

you can easily halve your average weekly dining bill. Remember, halved averages are the best kind of averages.

Breakfast is the most important meal of the day. But do you have time to cook it, eat it, then clean up after yourself before you head off to work? Of course not. Better to spend that time sleeping in, working on schemes to destroy your enemies or practising your hatred of the lower classes.

But you also don't want to be wasting money by buying breakfast every morning. So instead, as you walk to work, confidently stride into any luxury hotel and fill a plate of food from the breakfast buffet. With a bold enough demeanour, the maitre'd will usually be too yellow to ask you for a room number, but even if they do, you can easily invent one. Remember: Don't go for numbers too high too often. That just draws attention to yourself. Stick to something sensible, like, say, 127.

Luxury hotels, by the way, also provide the best public lavatories. Maintaining bowel regularity is the key here, so be sure to grab high fibre cereal from the buffet, along with prunes. Beans will also serve you well (I call this 'legume theory', a play on words too clever for those Australian bastards and other dim-witted folk to follow). The less often you have to use your bathroom at home, the less often you have to clean it.

After breakfast, meet up with an underling from work to get yourself half-price takeaway coffee for the office. Here's how to do it. Have your underling (let us call him 'Harold') order a coffee. Let him pay for it, but when the barista calls out his name, *you* go to the counter to claim it. Cafe staff are an uneducated and unruly lot and will never notice you weren't the one who made the order. But a few minutes later, Harold can complain he never got his coffee and they'll have no choice but to make him another one.

Easy. With this simple tactic, you have two coffees for the price of one, and the day has just begun. Harold will probably want to take it in turns to pull off this trick, but at least once a week you can 'forget' your wallet and have him cover you more often. It's still worth his while and, on average, you'll end up paying even *less* than half-price. And if your underling refuses to pay short for coffee in this manner, get rid of him and find another who'll more readily do your bidding.

Speaking of half-price deals, keep an eye out for two-for-one vouchers for any cafes and restaurants near your workplace. Once you find one, tell a work colleague you've never really liked (eg the Nawab of Pataudi) that you'll take care of the tedious bloody nonsense of picking up lunch. Collect the money from him, then use the voucher to get *your* meal for free.

Can't find any vouchers? There's usually plenty of food in the office refrigerator. Moreover, the containers are often labelled so you'll know who to avoid afterwards. It may not be a clever tactic, but it's a bloody effective one. And if you can make a little Australian show-off bastard go hungry in the process, all the better.

Finally, if you need to step into the grocery store on the way home to pick up food for dinner, always use the self checkout. Remember, nobody can see the difference between organic foods and regular foods. Put the best quality on the scales, but pay only for the worst. The so-called 'best' food isn't that much better anyway, and you'll feel immense satisfaction at bringing its numbers down to the same level as the rest.

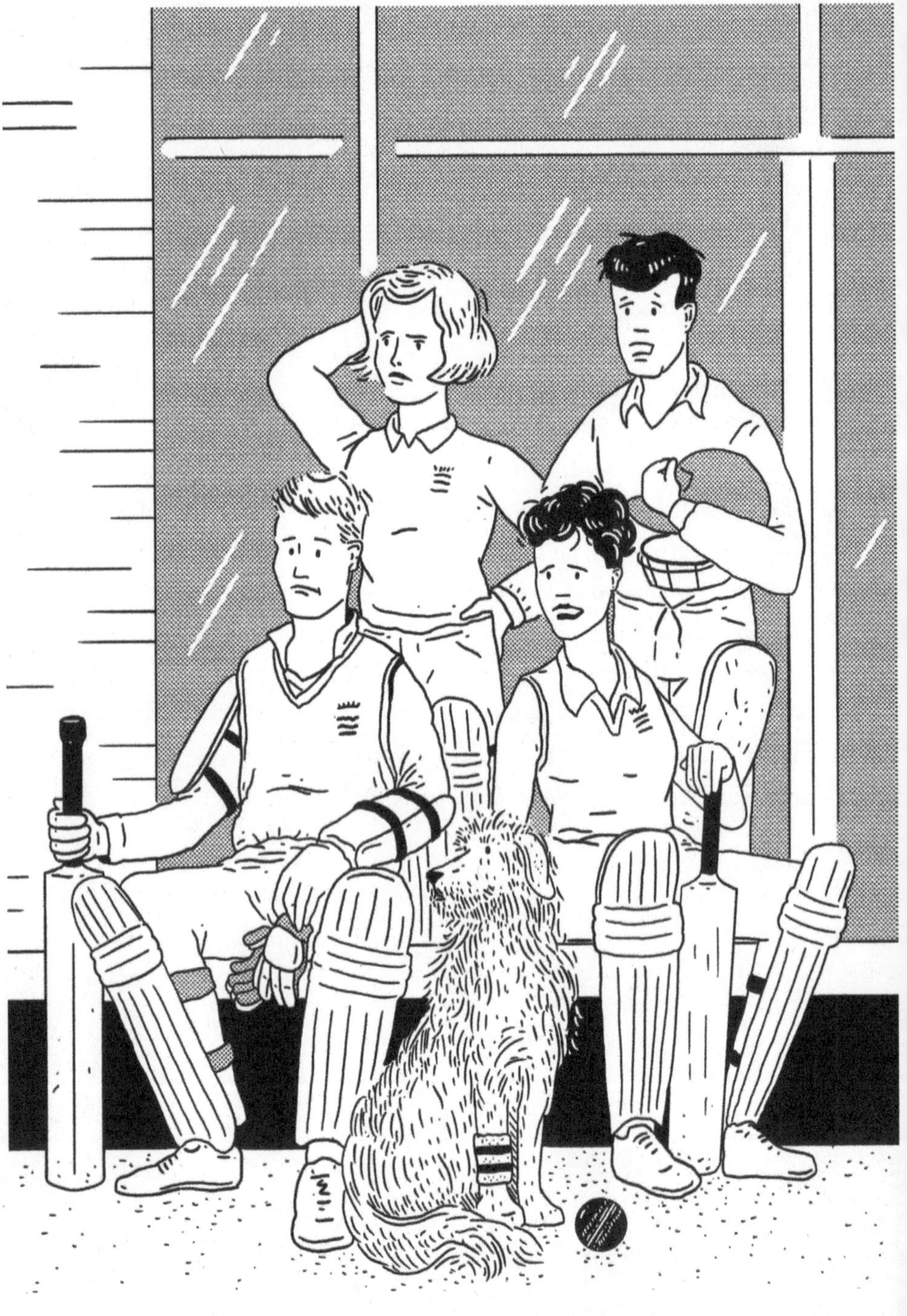

Struck Down by a Queer Spell

**AN EXCERPT FROM 'FIVE ARE DISMISSED WITHOUT SCORING',
BY ENID BLYTON**

*Remember the time Enid Blyton's beloved children's heroes were
selected to make their Test debut? Of course you do.*

Dick looked through the window. He could see Julian had made his way through the hidden tunnel and emerged on the ground. "He looks so peculiar in that helmet," said George.

Dick laughed. "He sure does," he said. All the padding Julian was wearing on his legs and hands and chest were comical enough. He'd even shoved what appeared to be a turtle down his trousers. But on his head he wore something that looked like a miner's helmet without the light.

Dick smiled at the thought. Imagine! Julian labouring down the mines, in the dark, like a working class boy, rather than spending his summer holidays making his Test debut for England. Ha!

Suddenly, Anne pointed and shrieked. "Is that a pirate!" she exclaimed. Timmy growled fiercely.

"Don't be so daft, Anne," said Dick. "There are no pirates at Lord's." Although, as he looked closer, he had to admit that the man did look very much like a freebooting corsair, with his beastly moustache and cold, merciless eyes.

"He's something far worse than a pirate," revealed George, grimly. "That's an Australian fast bowler."

"Ugh," said Anne. "He sounds ghastly." She went off to make some cucumber sandwiches and scones. They were all famished and tea was still thirty minutes away.

What had they gotten themselves into, wondered Dick to himself. When Aunt Fanny had been appointed the head coach of the England cricket team, they'd all been so happy for her. They'd even thrown a party, where they'd had cupcakes and lemonade and run something called a 'beep test'. Aunt Fanny had joked that if the team lost the first couple of Test matches, the children might be forced to help out. It had all seemed so far-fetched and silly back then.

But now here they were, all making their Test debuts, with the Ashes on the line.

Anne shrieked again. "The pirate's going for Julian!" she said, almost dropping the tray of food.

"I told you, he's *not* a pirate," said Dick.

"He *is* going for him, though," said George.

And so he was. The man was running straight at Julian. Small steps to begin with. But then longer and faster ones as he got closer.

"I hope Julian knows how to use that bat," said Dick, concerned.

"He will," said Anne. "He must," she whispered to herself. George hugged Timmy close.

Before anybody could see what had happened, the man flung the ball at Julian in a flurry of arms and legs and moustaches. The ball bounced in front of Julian then up at his head. He fended it away desperately with his bat, straight into the hands of a bearded man with long and untidy hair, standing in close.

"Golly," said Dick. "That was nasty."

"I'm going out there," declared George.

"Oh no you're not," said Dick.

"Just you try and stop me," said George.

And before Dick knew what was happening, George had disappeared out the door and down the same secret tunnel that Julian had found earlier.

"I'm frightened," said Anne.

"There, there," said Dick, holding her hand. "No need to be scared. I'm here."

"And I'm here, too!" said Julian, as he walked back into the dressing room, unstrapping his pads.

"Julian!" shouted Anne, giving him a fierce hug. "You're safe."

"Yes," said Julian. He told them about everything that had happened out in the middle. The excited crowd. The frightful Australians. The short ball he would ordinarily have stepped inside and hooked for an imperious six had he not been undone by inconsistent bounce on a poorly prepared track.

"Darn that rotten curator!" said Dick. "He's ruined everything."

Suddenly, there was a crash and another roar. Dick peered out the window.

"Is it George?" asked Julian, unable to bring himself to look.

Dick nodded. George's stumps had been destroyed by another ball from the Australian pirate.

"Crumbs!" swore Julian. "We need a consolidating partnership here." He put a hand on Dick's shoulder. "Just see out the over, Dick," he said.

"I—I'll try," said Dick, hesitantly.

Dick grabbed a bat and made his way down the tunnel and into a long room. Somehow, in all the excitement, he must have become confused, for he soon found himself down in the basement lavatories.

"Taken a wrong turn, have you, lad?" said a fat old man, smartly dressed except for a dreadful striped tie and jacket.

"Yes, sir," said Dick. He was about to ask for directions, but the man had already entered a stall.

Dick fled. By the time he had retraced his steps, he found Anne returning down the tunnel, with Timmy trotting along beside her.

"What happened?" said Dick.

"I'll tell you what happened," said Julian, poking his head around the door. "You were timed out, then Anne was caught behind from her very first ball. Then, in the next over, Timmy was trapped leg before wicket."

"Well," said Dick. "He *does* have two more legs than the rest of us!"

Anne giggled at that. Timmy barked happily.

"Some of those Australians had real potty mouths too," said George.

"I know," said Anne. "And why had so many of them been staying over with Mother last night?"

"Never mind that," said Julian. "With Timmy's dismissal, we've just lost 7 wickets for 19 runs and collapsed to 114 all out."

"Oh, bother," said Dick. Aunt Fanny was going to be furious.

Still, at least Timmy had become the first dog to ever play Test cricket. And only the fourth player ever to urinate on the stumps on debut. So that was something.

An Amazing Day Off

AN EXCERPT FROM 'FINE WINES AND FINE LEGS'
BY HENRY BLOFELD

Henry Blofeld is a veteran cricket broadcaster renowned for his natty dress sense and Wodehousian phrases. Here's an excerpt from his lost memoir of the 2006-07 Ashes series.

After a wholly unmemorable breakfast at the hotel, I shared a cab to the ground with Geoffrey Boycott. I dropped him off outside the media entrance, telling him I had an errand to run and that I'd return to the commentary box shortly.

In fact, I had no intention whatsoever of returning. Both teams had already racked up 500 runs on a lifeless pitch. Rather than spend the final day of the Second Test watching England secure the draw with some leisurely batting practice out in the middle, I had resolved to instead undertake a relaxing excursion around one of my very favourite Australian cities.

Firstly I popped over to the Adelaide Real Tennis Club[1]. In a moment of what could only be described as overconfident folly, I'd agreed to a game against David Gower at the Royal Melbourne Club during the Fourth Test.

---

1 Editor's note: As any Real Tennis enthusiast would know, there's no such club in Adelaide. Whether this part of the tale is misremembered or misplaced should be considered an exercise for the enthusiastic reader.

As a result I needed to get in some practice, if only so the moment of folly could be retrospectively downgraded to a status of 'poorly thought through'. I played a couple of sets against the peculiarly distracted club president before winning comfortably with a skilful hazard chase in the second set.

Afterwards, I caught up with some of the other members for some scones and a cup of tea, at which point we talked about their plans for the renovation of the club.

"I do hope you don't alter the service end of the court too much," was my main suggestion. "It has so much character."

"Warne!" spluttered the club president, who'd been sitting in the corner of the room, conducting what I assumed to be renovation research on his laptop.

His outburst caused me to take a second glance at the court. Yes, the flooring *was* a little worn, but a third glance suggested one could also look upon it as priceless patina. I fear that Australia, being a country still in the earlier flushes of youth, is not as comfortable as other, less youth-flushed, nations might be with the charms of more venerable decor. Perhaps even an establishment as otherwise meritorious as the Real Tennis Club was not immune to such a blinkered perspective.

I bade farewell and set off to meet Barry Richards for lunch. I ordered the most spectacular 2005 Henschke Croft Chardonnay, which I paired with a seafood risotto with spring vegetables and the two of us spent a lovely few hours reminiscing about our salad days. The only disappointing aspect of the meal was the distractible and unfocused waiting staff, always scurrying back to the kitchens where I could glimpse them gathering around the transistor radio and laughing. It was intensely irritating behaviour and one reflected in the magnitude of my gratuity. Or, indeed, the absence thereof.

After lunch, I strolled through Rundle Mall, where I noticed the stores emptying out, and the locals excitedly chattering to themselves about something or other as they rushed off. I took this as a cracking opportunity to do some shopping of my own, without worrying about autograph hunters or other riffraff. It was while I was shopping for a truly splendid cravat that the assistant tried to entice me into conversation about the Test.

"Hard to believe what's happening in the Test," he said, excitedly.

I smiled to myself. Yes, I suppose to the average Australian, ill-educated in the twists and turns of our beautiful game, England's ability to recover from a First Test drubbing to dominate this Second Test *would* be somewhat unbelievable.

"Never underestimate the mental strength of the British," I said, offering a knowing wink.

"Ha!" he replied. "Nice one."

After I purchased the cravat and a simply smashing smoking jacket, I made my way back to an ice cream vendor I'd spied earlier. Alas, to my dismay, I saw that the vendor was closing his shop early. I caught him just as he was locking up and enquired about the prospect of a cone.

"Sorry, mate," he said. "Pigeon's got the last and I'm off to see the chase."

He scurried away before I could enquire any further. Chasing after ice-cream eating pigeons? Incomprehensible. On reflection, it was surely yet another example of the kind of baffling Australian slang of which I've never been able to make head nor tail. Like 'fair suck of the sauce bottle' or 'classless meritocracy'.

Instead, I visited Haigh's Chocolates, where I purchased some peppermint crunch on which to nibble as I searched for a new pair of slacks to make their debut in Perth.

The afternoon wore on. By the time the last crunch was nibbled, and the last nibble crunched, I had several bags of shopping under my arms. As I pondered in which restaurant I might dine, I couldn't help but notice crowds of people gathered around television sets in the department stores.

I shook my head sadly as I walked past the vacuous throng. The fresh air of a perfect summer afternoon did not merely beckon them, it performed an erotic dance of seduction. And yet these youngsters remained sadly oblivious to its charms.

Suddenly, a shout went up.

"Hussey!" shouted a man sporting a beard that knew no boundaries.

I was aghast at his crudity. I tried to find the woman he was insulting but to no avail. Certainly, none of the television-addled women in the crowd seemed to be taking offence. There was instead laughter and cheering at the man's crassness.

With the opportunity for chivalry swept away by their merriment, I instead made my way to a curiously deserted restaurant, where I ordered a glass of champagne from the bar. I sipped upon it as I attempted the Telegraph crossword.

"What a great Test," said a hoop-earringed woman sitting across the bar from me.

I smiled and nodded. "Very much so," I replied.

What a marvellous and contradictory nation Australia was. And, in particular, this beautiful city. In one moment, I found myself in despair at the boorish elements on display. And yet here, in the next, its denizens were exhibiting appreciation at the subtle nuances of a drawn Test that promised to set up a closely-fought Ashes series.

Adelaide, you truly are amazing.

The Rise of Speed

**AN EXCERPT FROM 'THE QUICKS AND THE DEAD:
AN EXPOSE OF THE AUSTRALIAN FAST BOWLERS' CARTEL'**

*Thanks to investigative journalism at its very best
from the anonymous author, the mysterious Deep Third Man,
we read the chilling truth behind the rise of the
Australian Fast Bowlers' Cartel.*

At 2:15pm on March 1, 2014, Michael John Clarke was the victim of a Morne Morkel hit in Cape Town. Morkel had long been rumoured to be a kingpin in the South African fast bowler's cartel, and Clarke was not the first batsman to succumb to the behemoth's supply of speed.

But as a victim of South African speed—also known on the street by slang terms such as 'pace' or, distressingly, 'wheels'—Clarke was no innocent. Far from it. In fact, it was Clarke who had brought his own fast bowlers' cartel onto the South Africans' turf and instigated the speed war in which he was now embroiled. Clarke's pace purveyors—whom I can exclusively reveal to be Mitchell Johnson, 32, from Perth, Western Australia, Ryan 'No Knees' Harris, 34, from Brisbane, Queensland and James Pattinson, 23, from Melbourne, Victoria—were facing off against those from South Africa: Morkel and the infamous enforcer Dale Steyn.

Steyn's supply of speed, in particular, was said to be potent enough to knock over a rhino. To confront Steyn on his own territory showed how brazen the Australians had become.

But the risk for Clarke and the rest of the Australian Cricket Family was not without its rewards. The victorious cartel would be able to lay claim to the control of cricket addicts throughout the southern hemisphere, and that was a temptation too powerful to resist.

The effects of speed had swept through Australia in the six months prior to this 2014 foray into South Africa. It had been the moustachioed, tattooed Johnson who had been pushing the most addictive doses down the supply chain. Long known to the authorities as a minor supplier of mostly harmless and wayward varieties of pace with little to no effect on batsmen, Johnson had previously only found success with a speed/crack hybrid, and even then usually only in Perth, Western Australia.

But in recent months Johnson had developed a new and potent strand of pace. Despite the warnings of Clarke, neither England tourists nor Australian spectators were sufficiently prepared to resist the allure of Johnson's speed.

The impact of his pace was immediate, and when the Australian fast bowlers' cartel eventually proved too strong for their South African nemeses in 2014, there was nothing to stop the spread of pace throughout the land.

Speed was soon seen on every street corner in Australia. Four years on, at the time of this writing, its insidious effects are still being felt, as a once-proud nation struggles to extricate itself from pace's pernicious grip.

Johnson and Harris are long gone, of course—even the most terrifying dealers in speed will, sooner or later, find themselves whacked. And Pattinson is missing, presumed suffering from stress fractures. But others have taken their place.

The speed of brazen upstart Mitchell Starc, 28, from Sydney, New South Wales, has proven to be as addictive as that of his namesake predecessor. Perhaps even more so, with a source at Cricket Australia informing me that a striking pink pace variant is now regularly dealt just outside the central business district of Adelaide, South Australia, often after dark.

Another prominent pace supplier from Sydney is 27-year-old Josh Hazlewood. Also known as the notorious Hazleberg, aka The One Who Ends Knocks, he is rumoured to have developed his pace in a hidden super-lab, deep beneath an otherwise unremarkable cricket academy, which would account for the clinical precision of his speed.

But most disturbing of all the speed merchants is Pat Cummins, 24, who has been dealing in pace since he was a teenager. For a time, it seemed as if Cummins had gotten out of the speed game and reintegrated into society, but his recent re-emergence as a member of the Sydney triad has led many opponents of pace and its effects to despair. What hope is there for the future of Australia when a kid such as Cummins, with so much going for him, can be so easily caught up in the speed industry?

Australia has had outbreaks of speed all throughout its cricket history. In the 1970s, Lillee and Thomson infamously provided pace of such potency that the taste for undiluted speed spread as far afield as the Caribbean, where fast bowlers' cartels went on to dominate the region for the better part of two decades. This trend was perhaps captured best in the lightly fictionalised accounts of the American writer Mario Puzo, most notably in his best-seller 'The Lloydfather'.

Before that, Ray Lindwall and Keith Miller had dealt in speed in the quiet suburbs of 1950s Australia, much to the shock of a nation still recovering from the Second World War.

And, of course, in more recent decades, there had been Brett Lee, Jason Gillespie, Merv Hughes, Craig McDermott and others, all of whom had held cricket fans in the ruinous thrall of speed for a brief time.

But in all those previous instances, Australia's addiction to pace had faded away almost as quickly as it had arrived.

This time feels different. This time the speed feels as if it's here to stay. For as I will reveal, the tentacles of speed addiction have now reached to the very top of Cricket Australia.

But while it is easy to despair, it should be remembered that at 2:17pm on March 1, 2014, Michael Clarke stood back up in Cape Town and faced Morne Morkel again. Clarke's shoulder had been fractured, but despite this he marked his crease once more. He went on to make an undefeated 161.

The war on speed can be won. The fast bowlers' cartels can be beaten. We must stand up to them.

The Battle of Eden

AN EXCERPT FROM 'DANGEROUS BLADES AND MAGICAL SPELLS' BY GEORGE R. R. BAILEY

Here's one of the most famous battles in Bailey's epic sword and sorcery series, now a smash hit cable television show.

King B-Mac stood before his men. The West Island forces led by Old Pup would soon meet them on their shores. That much had been presaged by his seers after mystic consultation with the Flames of Foreboding, and also the official ICC 2015 World Cup schedule.

Old Pup and his men meant to conquer the world, just as they had done under the Mad Punter King and, before him, the Great Waugh-Lord. There were some who spoke of an even earlier conqueror—a Border Swordsman—but these were whispers of a forgotten era.

The West Islanders were fearsome and ferocious. Their general, the Old Pup, was renowned as a master tactician, full of sly schemes and fields of funkiness.

King B-Mac knew he had to fan the hopes of his men. To charge them for battle.

"My brothers, I am not so out of touch that I do not know the trepidation you feel," he began. "The West Islanders are a foe without

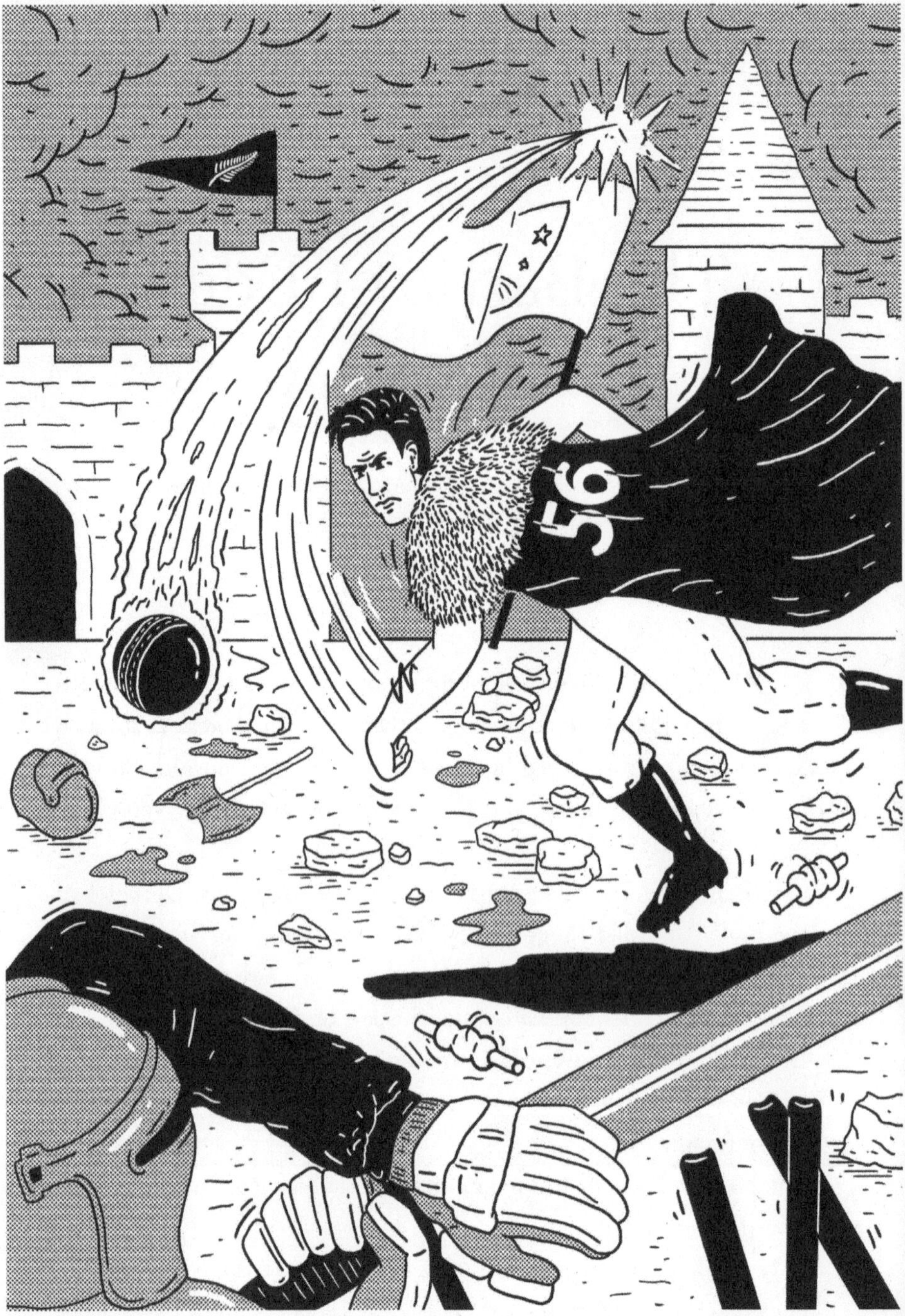
56

measure. David Who Warns. Mitchell, Son of John. Sir Watson of the Front Pad. These are names that inspire dread among mortal men."

He stared into their wary eyes.

"But I look around the men standing before me, and I say nay," he continued. "We should not fear the West Islanders."

He paused and met the gaze of Prince Kane, The Chosen One. His finest soldier.

"I say, the West Islanders should fear us."

A small smile came from Prince Kane. And muttering grew among the men.

"What of Aaron the Finch?" said the king, a sudden sneer on his face. "Can he fly fast enough to combat an attack from our own Timothy of the South?"

"Nay!" came several voices in reply.

"The Old Pup? Can his ailing back straighten enough to avoid the wiles of Daniel the Veteran?"

Now even more voices. "Nay!"

"And can Maxwell the Mad conjure the wits to combat a mystical Boult of Lightning?"

Every man now responded as one. "Nay!"

"There may come a day-night ODI when our courage fails," continued King B-Mac. "But it is not this day-night ODI. This day-night, we fight. Let us inflict the terror on the West Islanders that they inflict on all others."

He paused for dramatic effect.

"For. We. Wear. The. Black. Cap."

And with an almighty roar, his men surged onto The Park of Eden to do battle.

By the time the initial melee had ended, the West Island forces had been decimated. It had taken but 32.2 overs to repel them and the Old Pup's warriors had secured a mere 151 runs as recompense for their losses.

Sensing victory, King B-Mac led the secondary charge. He would vanquish the West Islanders himself. With thrashing blade and crazed intent, he repelled the spell of Mitchell, Son of John. And in a mere four-and-twenty balls, the king alone had claimed just shy of one-third of the victory target.

He returned to his quarters, satisfied. The tide of battle had been set. It was now but a matter of time until Old Pup's men were routed.

The first word of trouble came from Martin Two-Toes. "There is a counter-attack, my liege," he reported. "Led by Mitchell—"

"Impossible," said King BMac. "I defeated the Son of John myself."

"It is not Mitchell the Elder doing the damage. Nor is it Mitchell of Swamp Castle. It is Mitchell the Younger. Of House Starc."

"House Starc," muttered the king. He had heard tell of the Starcs gathering strength. Of a betrothal to Alyssa, niece of Ian, of House Healy that would unite their kingdoms.

He had always perceived the union of Houses Starc and Healy as a quandary to be dealt with in some future season. Mayhap he had underestimated Mitchell The Younger.

Bah. It mattered not. Victory was in their grasp. Despite the raw power of the Starc lad, the battle was almost done. What could one man do?

And yet the reports kept coming from the field. Almost more than the king could follow. Of thunderbolts too fast for human eyes to see, hurled with a venom and accuracy beyond the imagination of even the most wild-eyed of fools.

Ross the Taylor and Grant-Meister Elliott had seen their castles destroyed by him in twin strikes.

Now the castles of Adam the Milliner and Timothy of the South had also been destroyed by Mitchell the Younger, who spoke the terrifying language of the body as he roared his cruel delight.

It was impossible to behold. Lord Starc had singlehandedly dragged the West Islanders to the brink of victory in a battle where victory brinks should have been well outside of single-handed dragging range.

And yet on the field of battle remained Prince Kane, who even the Old Crowe regarded as the Black Caps' finest ever wielder of the blade. Now, in their darkest hour, he showed his silken prowess yet again. For with one almighty blow, he ended the battle, earning victory for his men. The West Islanders retreated, back to their sprawling, garish lands.

It had been a hard-fought triumph for King B-Mac and his men. If fortune held they would next meet the West Islanders on their own lands. The victor that day would rule the world and sup from the Iron Cup.

But to succeed on that day, King B-Mac now knew he would need to best young Lord Starc. Winter was coming, but he would find the time to ruminate on his stratagems.

It's The End of the World Cup as We Know It

AN EXCERPT FROM 'TO BE THE TWELFTH'
BY ANDY BICHEL

In an acclaimed autobiography, the paceman reveals the heartache at losing his beloved 12th man spot during the 2003 World Cup.

Although I'd established myself as a world class twelfth man at Test level, I still dreamed of carrying the drinks at a World Cup. 'Heals' (Ian Healy) had always talked about the wicketkeeper being the drummer in the band. To me, the twelfth man was an even more important role—the roadie for the band. After all, if the drummer doesn't show up, a band can always use a drum machine. But if the roadie doesn't show up, what are they going to do? There's no such thing as a roadie machine. (Unless you count artificially intelligent forklifts, which, frankly, I never have.)

I wanted nothing more than to be the roadie of our 2003 World Cup campaign and got my chance in the very first game against Pakistan.

I was pleased with how I performed in the role. 'Roy' (Andrew Symonds) made 143 not out and I felt in the zone.

It's hard to describe what it's like to be so on top of the game—to always have a new bat or a new helmet ready to go before the batsman even asks for it. But that's what it was like during that innings. I remember at one point late in Roy's knock when I'd run out a Port Elizabeth tide chart for him. He asked me whether I had a spare box if he needed one. I just gestured to a tell-tale bulge in my pocket.

He laughed. So did I. We were a perfect partnership that day and Australia won easily.

So you can imagine my surprise when 'Buck' (coach John Buchanan) and 'Punter' (captain Ricky Ponting) summoned me before the next match and told me that they'd decided to go with 'The Freak' (Ian Harvey) as 'twelfthie' against India.

"What? The Freak?" I said. Or words to that effect.

I was stunned. You could have knocked me over with a feather. (Buck disputed this, claiming that the tensile structure of a feather—even one from a large flightless bird such as an ostrich or a cassowary—wouldn't provide the focused force necessary to displace the centre of gravity of a man of my combined mass and surface area. Buck could sometimes be a dick about these kinds of things.)

And it soon became clear I wasn't just competing against The Freak. 'Hoggy' (Brad Hogg) and 'Mabo' (Jimmy Maher) twelfthed up against 'the Dutch' (the Netherlands) and 'Zimmers' (Zimbabwe) in the two games after that.

For the next game against Namibia, Mabo held his *l'homme douziemme* spot (as he now bizarrely insisted on calling it). Despite this, I was still hopeful that my drinks-carrying experience might get me the nod for the upcoming Super Six games and finals.

Those hopes were crushed in the final group game against 'the Poms' (England).

It started harmlessly enough. 'Pigeon' (Glenn McGrath) and 'Bing' (Brett Lee) opened the bowling and England raced along to '57/0' (0/57) after eight overs.

By this stage of the tournament, I was no longer even part of the dressing room unit. Instead, I was out on the field, along with the rest of the drinks-guzzlers.

Punter tossed me the ball and asked me to bowl. I still sometimes wake up in a cold sweat about what happened next.

Five deliveries into my first over, Nick Knight edged one to 'Marto' (Damien Martyn) and I had my first wicket. It was a terrible shot. Marto was the only wide slip, and Knight had guided it straight to him like an idiot.

If I'd thought that was a bad start, things got even worse in my second over. First I had Michael Vaughan feathering one behind for two from the first ball. And then I bowled England captain Nasser Hussain from the last. I caught him on the crease, seaming one into the off stump, straight past his rubbish defensive stroke.

I was distraught. My figures were now 3/3 from two overs. You don't get to be twelfth man with figures like that.

Pigeon stepped up and got rid of Marcus Trescothick in the next over. But when Paul Collingwood slashed like a lunatic at one of my wider deliveries to be caught behind, I knew it wasn't going to be my day.

Punter spelled me after six overs with the figures of 4/12. England, sensing my despair, refused to lose another wicket while I was out of the attack. Instead, Alec Stewart and Andrew Flintoff took them to 5/171 after forty overs.

That's when Punter threw the ball back to me. Flintoff almost immediately tried a mindless pull shot and skied one. 'Gilly' (Adam Gilchrist) took a simple catch to give me a five-wicket haul.

Stewart then inexplicably missed one and was bowled in my next over.

I wrapped up my spell with Ashley Giles stupidly chipping one to 'Bevo' (Michael Bevan) at mid-off to give me the dream-crushing figures of 7/20.

If my bowling had severely damaged my chances of dozeneering again in this tournament, my batting sealed my fate.

By the time I came to the crease, England had us 8/135 in the 38th over, chasing a target of 205. For a moment I dared to hope. Maybe, just maybe, my bowling figures might be overlooked in the aftermath of a shock loss to England.

Instead, Bevo did his thing and the two of us put on 73 undefeated runs to win the game with a couple of balls to spare.

I was gutted.

Still, credit where it's due. Mabo's twelfthing was sublime throughout our partnership. I remember when he brought out gloves for Bevo at the end of the 43rd over. 'Keep going,' he said. 'Don't get out.' And so we did, and didn't.

What Mabo had worked out was that if either one of us were dismissed, Pigeon would be in next. And Pigeon couldn't bat for shit. Assessing the match situation like that and passing it on to the men in the middle is excellent twelfth-manning. I knew if I wanted my spot at the bottom of the team sheet back, I'd need to show Punter I could step up to Mabo's level.

But, alas, I wouldn't even get the opportunity. My performance against England (7/20 and 34 not out) had ensured that. Instead, I would feature in every game for the rest of the tournament and play an integral on-field role in an unprecedented, undefeated campaign.

My World Cup dream had become a nightmare. A nightmare featuring Jimmy Maher—easily the worst kind.

A Tiny Ripple of Hope

**THE INTRODUCTION TO 'I, PAD', SHANE WATSON'S
ANTI-LBW MANIFESTO**

*Shane Watson's magnificent thesis arguing against the
LBW Law won over many cricketing experts.*

It was Robert F Kennedy who said, "Each time a man stands up for an ideal, or acts to improve the lot of others, or strikes out against injustice, he sends forth a tiny ripple of hope, and crossing each other from a million different centres of energy and daring those ripples build a current which can sweep down the mightiest walls of oppression and resistance."

For too long, cricketers have been oppressed by the logically flawed and morally wicked 'leg before wicket' Law. Throughout my cricket career I have fought this heinous Law from within the system. Now, in semi-retirement, I can strike out against its injustice from the outside, without risk of compromise.

This manifesto is my tiny ripple of hope. It explains why the LBW Law is so terribly wrong and how its eradication will make cricket a far superior sport.

Join me in standing for the ideal of an LBW-free form of the game. Together we can sweep down this oppressive blight on the game.

In chapter one of this book we examine the history of the LBW Law and how its introduction enabled the middle and upper classes (the 'Gentlemen') to oppress both literal and metaphorical attempts by the working classes (the 'Players') to take necessary steps forward.

In chapter two we contemplate the logic of LBW in its current form. In particular, we analyse the required trigonometry to make the Law function. We then show that in a non-Euclidean geometry like that of the surface of an oblate ellipsoid such as the earth, any LBW decision must, at best, be an approximation and, hence, erroneous.

In chapters three through five we discuss controversial moments in cricket history (eg. Bodyline, the underarm delivery, pre-Duckworth Lewis rain rules). We posit that, in each case, the unquestioned application of the LBW Law was a more ethically strained element of the match than the headline-garnering incident.

In chapter six we examine leg byes. The logical inconsistency of the pads being allowed to substitute for the bat for the purpose of scoring runs but not for the defence of the stumps is challenged.

In chapters seven through nine we trace the development of ball-tracking software. We ponder the philosophical ramifications of subjunctive realities and why a decision made on the basis of ball-tracking necessarily presupposes the existence of a multiverse. In particular we examine the underlying hypothesis of a quantum-linked universe, identical to our own but for the absence of a batsman's legs. The argument is made that such a universe is inconsistent along multiple axes ('How does a batsman run?', 'What Darwinian principles could justify legless humans?', 'How does gravity work in a reality where a batsman existing from just the torso up can still float as if they possessed legs?', etc). From there we deduce that such a universe must, by construction, have very different laws of physics to our own. Can the tracking of a ball in a universe with different laws of physics to our own bear any relevance to the path of a ball in our universe? Of course not.

In chapters 10 and 11 we discuss the DRS system. How its embrace of the logically-flawed ball-tracking systems undermined its acceptance to right-thinking cricketers. And how the only sane response to such an inherently defective system is to ruthlessly satirise and mock it. We reveal how the author co-opted the 'T' sign for a review and turned it into a symbol of its own inherent absurdity, via the German phrase 'Torheit' (foolishness).

In chapters 12 through 15 we further trace the personal history of the author and his ongoing moral struggle against the LBW Law. How he was forced to work within the system if he wanted to change it. How each triumph—the many centuries, captaining his nation in all formats, the multiple Allan Border Medals, the many controversies—was carefully examined to ensure he never lost sight of his true path and that he was never tempted into acceptance of the game's erroneous status quo.

Chapter 16 imagines cricket freed from the yoke of the LBW Law. How this single change to the game's Laws would create multi-dimensional players, equally skilled with bat and pad. How it would therefore open a path for athletes to transition from the world of football and ensure the sport of cricket a bright and powerful future.

Chapter 17 is a call to action to cricket players, fans, administrators, umpires and scorers. The preceding chapters of the book have shown the LBW Law to be an outdated, broken and conceptually flawed blight upon our great game. Now it's time to come together and repeal it.

● ● ●

I trust by the time you finish reading this manifesto, you'll embrace my argument and join me in the resistance. While it is all but too late for my career, it's not too late for others.

Together we can sweep down the oppressive wall of Law 36.1 and guide cricket to a new and better era.

The Sights and the Sounds

What do they know of cricket broadcasting who only cricket broadcasting know?

AN EXCERPT FROM 'BEHIND A BOUNDARY' BY J L R PREVITERA

Joe The Cameraman's memoir is by common consensus the greatest book about cricket cameramen ever written. Here, Joe attempts to straddle the divide between cameramen and commentators.

I left cricket broadcasting school having graduated first in my year in both commentary and cameramanning. At this time, I had two paths into the coverage of the game vying for my attention, and here the trouble began.

One of these paths was cameraman, the career of the visual artist. Class did not matter so much to them as silence. They had founded themselves on the principle that if you wanted to be involved in the television broadcasting of cricket, you were there to show the game. If you wanted to talk about cricket, go find a place in radio, was their credo.

The other path was commentator. This was generally considered to be a lower-class pursuit so limiting that even untrained former cricketers could find their way to a microphone. To many at this time, hearing was self-evidently an inferior sense to sight, and there was little more to be said, or shown, on the matter.

The reader is here invited to make up his mind. If for him all this is 'not cricket broadcasting', then he should take friendly warning and go in peace (or in wrath).

I had gone to school with many of the cameramen. But I was also clearly a commentator. I would offer my thoughts on the game with the scarcest of provocation, and I know that some of the more established cameramen considered this tendency to be problematic. But the veteran sports producer in charge of the broadcasting unit had no patience with all that foolishness. He approached me in a roundabout manner: "Well, I hear you want to join us," he said, with a big smile and an even bigger headset.

I was unsure which path I wanted to take. Finally I decided to do what even then I rarely did—I decided to ask advice. I spoke to the father of a close friend, a commentator himself, but one openly contemptuous of these sensual lines. He listened gravely before advising me to take the opportunity to become a cameraman. "Take the opportunity to become a cameraman, Joe," he said, which couldn't have been clearer.

Not altogether convinced, but reassured, I joined the fraternity of cameramen and spent many years transmitting the game to viewers all around the world.

But my decision cost me a great deal. Faced with the fundamental divisions in the televising of cricket, I had gone to the camera. Cutting myself off from the commentary side had delayed my broadcasting development for years. But no one could see that then, least of all me.

● ● ●

Once in a blue moon, ie once in a lifetime, a man is handed on a plate a gift from heaven. I was handed mine in November, 1999.

Throughout my career I had grown to realise that one day I would be forced to face reality and finally straddle that inglorious divide between cameraman and commentator. But that day had never seemed to arrive.

As it happened, and not that I knew it at the time, I was waiting for Scott Muller.

Could he bowl? Could he throw? They're the questions I'm so often asked. And the answer is as obvious as you might expect: of course he could. He was an international cricketer, for goodness sake.

My criticisms of Muller were not intended to be taken at face value, but rather as a gesture of solidarity to my commentary brothers. We were on the brink of a new millennium. Even if there had ever been a rational basis for social division based on who dealt in vision and who dealt in sound, its time had long since passed.

Muller's wayward throw was an opportunity to take a stance. And take it emphatically. The class hierarchy that separates cameraman and commentator is—or, rather, should be—a fiction. It is a chasm that should not exist, like a day one WACA crack just outside the line of off stump.

I was, in my mind, the WACA curator of cricket broadcasting equality, watering the square containing the twin pitches of commentary and camera work with my own paired critiques of Muller's game, in the hope it would help seed the couch grass of unification that would bind our collective clay together, to deliver a broadcast full of the true bounce, pace and carry of genuine egalitarianism.

Alas, the reality underlying this admittedly convoluted analogy was somewhat different. Because in the media hubbub that followed, I was designated primarily by one appellation.

I was 'Joe the Cameraman'.

My place in the social strata, it seemed, would not be so easily shifted. But as far as I was concerned, the battle had just begun.

The Stunning Secret Origin of Banner-Man!

Banner-Man is cricket's first and greatest superhero.
Mint editions of the first issue of the Banner-Man comic book
are worth approximately 2/3 of a million dollars.

YES IT'S BANNER-MAN! TEST CRICKET'S FIRST RUN-SCORER, FIRST SCORER OF FIFTY, CENTURY AND 150, FIRST MAN TO RETIRE HURT IN A TEST AND...

... THE HOLDER OF TEST CRICKET'S OLDEST RECORD OF HIGHEST PERCENTAGE OF RUNS SCORED IN A COMPLETED INNINGS.

WHEREVER THERE IS CRIME, WICKEDNESS OR ILL-DIRECTED MISCHIEF ...

... BANNER-MAN WILL STOP ROUGHLY 2/3 OF IT

FOR HE IS BANNER-MAN, 67.3% OF CRICKET'S GREATEST HERO! PROUDLY DISPLAYING THE MESSAGE OF TRUTH, JUSTICE AND (REDACTED).

Introduction to International Cricket: a Timeline

AN EXCERPT FROM 'LET ME INTRODUCE YOU TO MY ASSOCIATES'
BY TIM MILLER, ASSOCIATE CRICKET CORRESPONDENT, ESPNCRICINFO

How do we give as many nations full international status as quickly as possible? Tim Miller has the answers.

By now it's obvious that the ICC needs to give official Test, ODI and T20I status to as many countries as possible.

But we don't want to bring these nations into the fold only to have them struggle for decades. The key to avoiding this fate is to fast-track the newly inducted nation through the entire history of cricket and bring them up to international speed as quickly as possible.

Our internal modelling suggests that the ICC could create a high-level cricketing nation within a year simply by using an accelerated touring program and partnering with an established Full member. As an example, here's how Australia could help Botswana establish itself as a fully-fledged international cricket nation.

JANUARY

After Australia finish their international summer against an existing Test nation, they will move straight into a one-off Test against Botswana in Canberra.

At the end of the match, the losing side will be encouraged to destroy a piece of cricketing equipment (eg burn the bails, snap a stump-cam in half, slash the shoelaces off Mitchell Starc's shoes to create The Slashes) and, going forward, use the remains as a symbol of the great rivalry between Australia and Botswana.

FEBRUARY

Late February will see controversy threaten the bonds that tie together the great cricketing nations of Australian and Botswana.

In an attempt to level the playing field between the two nations during an ODI series, Botswana's captain will devise a scheme to ruthlessly bounce the Australian batsmen. This violation of the Spirit of Cricket will ideally force the home side to send a telegram of complaint to the powerful but dismissive Botswana Cricket Club.

MARCH

The ODI series will end in further discord when the Australians exploit a little-known playing condition to secure a controversial win against the plucky Botswana side.

Botswana will be permitted to complain about the Australians' underhanded play for the rest of their cricketing existence.

APRIL

A proposed visit by the Australians to Botswana for a T20 series will be disrupted when a significant number of Botswana's players are instead signed to a rebel tour of a boycotted cricketing region (ie a region in which Geoff Boycott resides, such as England or, more precisely, Yorkshire).

MAY

Just when Australia's T20 tour to face a severely weakened Botswana looks likely to end in farce, a rebel Botswanan billionaire will sign the best players from both sides in order to secure television rights.

As part of this television deal, a Rest of the World side will be hastily added to the tour. It will then be rescheduled as a 22-match tri-series, including a best of seven finals series.

JUNE

The second match of the finals between Australia and Botswana will explode in controversy when Botswana's finest spinner is called for chucking by an Australian umpire inexplicably presiding over the game.

A follow-up study by an official ICC biomechanics team will clear the spinner of any wrongdoing, only for doubts to linger when it's revealed that the team conducted their investigation on the wrong arm.

JULY

The seventh match of the finals series between Botswana and Australia will end with wild accusations of ball-tampering, triggering a riot from the home crowd and a controversial forfeit of the match.

Attempts to reschedule the match will be made, but by this stage everybody will be sufficiently fed up with one another that they'll all just head home instead.

AUGUST

While both sides take a break from one another, fresh conflict will arise with *Courier Mail* allegations that several of the preliminary games in the recent tri-series had been affected by spot-fixing.

An ICC anti-corruption unit will investigate and find 'no evidence' of the match-fixing, although they will note that the former Botswana captain's leather jacket is both 'pretty sweet' and 'climatologically unnecessary'.

SEPTEMBER

With an Australian tour on the horizon, Botswana's chances of success will be undermined by their most senior player (1 Test, 5 ODIs, 17 T20s) announcing his retirement from the game due to mental and physical exhaustion.

He will then immediately sign with multiple T20 franchises around the world, including the Hobart Hurricanes, the Quetta Gladiators and the Gaborone Gators.

OCTOBER

Botswana's tour of Australia will begin poorly when it is revealed that the Botswana wicket-keeper drunkenly head-butted a Marsh brother in (a) the nose and (b) a Perth nightclub.

NOVEMBER

Australia will win the First Test against Botswana at the Gabba following a questionable fourth innings DRS decision involving Hot Spot, Snicko and a camera-obscuring streaker.

A Botswana Cricket Club social media co-ordinator will be sacked after tweeting that the decision was '#bullshit'. She will be reinstated on appeal.

DECEMBER

Botswana's heroic Boxing Day Test victory will be overshadowed by reports of vicious Australian sledging in which the Botswana side were called 'a pack of —ers', 'cheating —ing —wits' and 'total Namibia wannabes'.

The Australian captain will insist that his team didn't cross the line and that the Botswana team should instead '——ing harden the — up, the —ing bunch of —ing —s'.

The year will therefore end with a Botswana team fully indoctrinated into the intricacies of international cricket and ready to take its place among the elite cricketing nations.

Christmas Comes Early

**THE INTRODUCTION TO 'OUT OF MY ED',
THE STUNNING TELL-ALL AUTOBIOGRAPHY OF ED COWAN**

*Perhaps you've always seen former Australian opener
Ed Cowan as a bookish, quiet, thoughtful cricketer.
You couldn't be more wrong.*

I was under the Torana, installing a forced induction charger when the missus poked her head into the garage.

"Ted!" she screeched, raising her voice to be heard above the Chisels belting out 'Khe Sanh' on the stereo. "Phone call."

"I'm busy," I shouted back. "Take a message."

"He says it's important," she yelled. "Some prick from Cricket Australia. Shannon Veryterry or something?"

"Bloody hell," I muttered. I pulled myself out from under the car, grabbed my pack of Winnie Blues and lit up a durry as I took the phone. What on earth was this about?

"Ed Cowan," I said, adopting my professional cricketer's voice.

"Ed," said the voice on the other end. "It's John Inverarity here, the Chairman of Selectors. I'm pleased to tell you that you've been selected to make your Test debut for Australia in the Boxing Day Test against India."

The ciggie fell from my mouth. Strike me pink.

"Thank you, John," I heard myself saying instead. "That's an absolute honour. I promise to represent Australia to the very best of my ability."

Strewth.

● ● ●

It didn't take long for the documentary wankers to show up for an interview about my selection. 'How does it feel?' 'You must be so proud'. The usual bullshit.

I'm not an imbecile. I knew what they were looking for. Shit, I'd known since I first signed on for their film. 'Death of a Gentleman' they were calling it, so you didn't have to be a brainiac to know they wanted fancy talk bullshit that the cricket intellectual dickheads could nod at and endlessly pontificate about.

Fine. Whatever. When I'd first heard about their little doco, I'd just been laid off from the Steggles factory and my band (The Daccas) had broken up. I needed the cash, so I'd ditched the flannies, covered up my Southern Cross tattoo and headed in to try out for the movie.

One of the directors, Jarrod Kimber, auditioned me first. The stupid baseball cap he always wore must have squeezed his brains out, because he totally fell for it. Nice guy, but dumb as dogshit. He took me over to the other director, Sam Collins, who also thought I was perfect for the movie.

The two of them had completely bought my schtick as 'Ed Cowan', University graduate, compost-recycling, politically correct, thinking man's cricketer. They hired me on the spot.

I took their advance, put a hundo through the pokies on the way home and didn't think much more of it.

I thought I could just appear in their little movie then get back to my life.

But things spun out of control from there. The doco guys introduced me to the Latin-spouting cricket writer Gideon Haigh. He also fell for the 'Ed Cowan' act, completely buying into this bookish, considerate, sensitive bullshit character I'd created.

Next thing I knew, old mate Haigh was talking me up in his newspaper column as a potential Test opener.

And then I heard that Cricket Australia was looking to get more left-wing thinkers into the team. Word was they liked to get as many left-wing/right-wing combos into the batting lineup as they could, to throw off opposition bowlers' political lines.

So, I continued the act. Went to town with it, in fact. What's your favourite book, Ed? Oh, I'd say, I can't decide between Stephen Hawking's 'A Brief History of Time' and 'Ulysses' by James Joyce.

Favourite movie? Akira Kurosawa's 'Rashomon'.

Favourite song? Pachelbel's Canon in D Major.

If Cricket Australia wanted a wine-drinking, book-reading, politically enlightened, chardy-drinking wanker to fill the gap left ever since Stuart MacGill retired, I'd be their man.

And now, here I was. Selected for Australia for the fucken Boxing Day Test. I shit you not.

Kimber and Collins went through their stupid interview questions about my selection. I gave them all the usual fancy talk I knew they wanted. Yep, I was proud to be playing for Australia. Dream come true. Nervous but excited. Blah, blah, blah.

They ate that shit up.

● ● ●

I ended up stuck playing the 'Ed Cowan' character for *years*. Right up until I retired. My mates would piss themselves laughing. 'Fuck me,

Ted,' they'd say, when I caught up with them at the local. 'What's all this players' union bullshit? Can't you wankers just play some cricket?'

And I'd just laugh and smash down another schooner.

It was a wild bloody ride, being 'Ed Cowan'. But it's about time you all read the real fucken story…

Listomania

AN EXCERPT FROM 'GREAT CRICKET LISTS, VOLUME 17'

For almost two decades the Great Cricket Lists series of books provided facts and trivia to cricket fans who had never heard of the internet. Volume 17 was no exception.

3 Reasons Why This Book is Better Than All 16 Previous Volumes Combined

1. No Tedious Stats – Ugh, how utterly boring is it to see list after list of numbers with that dreadful old show-off Bradman clogging things up everywhere?

2. Random Topics – We were going to structure the book thematically, then thought, 'Screw it. Just toss the lists in there in whatever order we came up with them.' Makes things more exciting, no?

3. More Meta – None of the previous volumes contained any lists referencing previous volumes of the Great Cricket Lists book series. This time we haven't made that mistake.

5 Australian Hat Trick Stories You've Heard Most Often (and one near hat-trick story)

1. **Merv Hughes** – Merv's hat-trick took three overs, two innings and two days to complete. Just like the retelling of it.

2. **Damien Fleming** – Fleming managed a hat-trick on Test debut. Impressive! Even more impressive is that the story of it is more often overshadowed by the story of the time Shane Warne dropped a catch to deny Flem a second hat-trick.

3. **Shane Warne** – Warne took his own hat-trick, against England. It was completed by David Boon taking a diving catch at short leg to dismiss Devon Malcolm. The twist? It was David Boon's birthday. The recitation of this hat trick story is now a Boxing Day Test tradition.

4. **Peter Siddle** – Speaking of birthdays, did you know Peter Siddle once took a hat-trick on his birthday? Of course you did.

5. **Glenn McGrath** – McGrath not only took a hat trick, he predicted he was going to do it, snared Brian Lara in the middle of it, and took his 300th Test wicket in the process. Okay. That's one worth hearing again.

8 Australian Test Cricketers with Initials BH
Only three more (plus a time machine) and we can field a team

1. Bill Howell
   (18 Tests, 1898-1904)
2. Bert Hopkins
   (20 Tests, 1902-09)
3. Bill Hunt
   (1 Test, 1932)
4. Bob Holland
   (11 Tests, 1984-86)
5. Brad Hogg
   (7 Tests, 1996-2008)
6. Brad Hodge
   (6 Tests, 2005-08)
7. Brad Haddin
   (66 Tests, 2008-15)
8. Ben Hilfenhaus
   (27 Tests, 2009-12)

12 Unbelievable, Yet True, Things Glenn Maxwell Has Done

1. Took a one-handed outfield catch while holding an ice cream.
2. Was fined and dropped from the team after complaining that he was batting below his wicket-keeper.
3. Responded to the lowest ever score for six wickets down in Sheffield Shield history (6/9) by scoring an 89-ball century, eventually making 127 in a total of 186.
4. Was dropped from the ODI team, then scored 145* (65) in his very next Australian innings, inexplicably opening the batting in a T20 match.
5. Broke his bat on his return to the Test side. And still scored a century.
6. Won an ODI against Pakistan by bowling a double wicket maiden for the final over of the match.
7. Left a post-match interview to give Sachin Tendulkar a hug.
8. Opened both the batting and bowling in his second Test, in which he was captained by Shane Watson.
9. Was signed for a million dollars in the IPL an hour after being dismissed for a golden duck in an ODI.
10. Reverse-swept the first ball of a T20 match for six.
11. Scored 96 while chasing down 295 against India in an ODI, brought the scores level with eight balls remaining, was caught trying to hit a six to bring up a century, then commentated the actual winning runs from the edge of the ground.
12. And, of course, left the first ball he faced in a BBL match and watched it crash into middle stump.

9 Batsmen Who Were Compared To Bradman

1. Neil Harvey
2. Sachin Tendulkar
3. Adam Voges
4. George Headley
5. Steve Smith
6. Norm O'Neill
7. Andy Ganteaume
8. Doug Walters
9. Donald Bradman

6 ODI Run Rate Rain Delay Target Adjustment Methodologies

1. **Simple Run Rate** – In the beginning, chasing teams just needed to match the first team's run rate regardless of overs or wickets lost. This was very simple. It was also very silly.

2. **Highest Overs** – The first attempt to adjust a target more fairly came via Richie Benaud's highest overs methodology. Here, as overs were lost for the chasing team, the lowest scoring overs from the team batting first were discarded from the total. Despite being slightly more complicated, this was considered OK right up until the evening South Africa suddenly had to make 22 from one ball in a World Cup semi-final.

3. **Duckworth/Lewis** – Enter the mathematicians. Frank Duckworth and Tony Lewis reframed the problem in terms of 'resources remaining' and came up with a much fairer way of adjusting targets. From this point, nobody other than huge nerds knew what was going on, but the nerds let players and umpires print out the results of their number-crunching and take those print-outs onto the field, so that was OK.

4. **Jayadevan's System (VJD)** – India had its own nerds, and one of them was V. Jayadevan, a civil engineer who came up with the VJD system.

It was even more complicated than Duckworth/Lewis and on very rare occasions gave different results—widely considered a welcome factor for losing teams, particularly losing Indian teams.

5. DLS – Analysing an upward trend in the letter counts for acronyms of target adjustment methodologies, Duckworth/Lewis added Professor Steven Stern to their algorithm, much like Crosby, Stills and Nash had done with Neil Young. The new methodology was now DLS, especially useful because it could be so easily confused with DRS.

6. WASP – Meanwhile, New Zealand nerds came up with a methodology named after an insect. They do things differently in New Zealand.

Cricket Goes Deluxe

AN EXCERPT FROM 'THE MARK NICHOLAS CRICKET CENTRE CATALOGUE' BY MARK NICHOLAS

The broadcaster and author made his first fortune selling cricket equipment. Here are highlights from one of his prestige catalogues.

This is one of the best compiled cricket kits I have ever seen. It is truly something very, very special. A genuinely magnificent display of the art of kit-making, which any modern cricketer will tell you is oh, so difficult.

Here's what this absolute beauty of a kit contains:

Jefford Edition Grade A English Willow Bat

This Jefford Edition Grade A English Willow Bat has been designed from the ground up to be all sweet spot. And it's oh so very, very sweet.

From the finest willow forests in North Hampshire, the Jefford Edition Grade A English Willow Bat is initially hand-carved by world-class cricket bat artisans. Just as Michelangelo did with the Statue of David, these master craftsmen unveil the bat within the willow, carefully removing the external non-bat elements to reveal the blade hidden deep inside. A brilliant piece of world-class whittling. Boy oh boy. Sumptuous.

Then, once the framework of the bat has been extracted from the initial willow, it moves to the Jefford finishing factory where it undergoes rigorous testing and refinement. The end result is a bat that combines the very best of both worlds: a hand-crafted wand of batting excellence for the most discerning batsmen in the game, honed to the finest millimetre-precise engineering specifications that ensure a maximal blend of power and balance. You little ripper.

Westminster Blue Ribbon Batting Pads

Yes! Yes! Yes! Leg byes will become a pleasure from the moment of impact to the completion of the run with these high-quality Westminster Blue Ribbon Batting Pads.

The Westminster Blue Ribbon Batting Pads feature the finest quality goose down to ensure maximum comfort and protection, while remaining so soft and supple that they hinder your running no more than an extra pair of socks.

Plus, for just £99 more, upgrade to the Westminster Blue Ribbon Batting Pads, Shane Watson Signature Edition, with buckles that contain inbuilt infrared sensors to calibrate the pad to the line of the stumps. Never again will you be unsure whether your front pad was outside the line of off stump. Brilliant stuff.

'A Beautiful Game' Prestige Batting Gloves

Shakespeare once wrote, 'O, that I were a glove upon that hand, That I might touch that cheek!'. Your team-mates will be uttering similar phrases when they see you strap on these 'A Beautiful Game' Prestige Batting Gloves.

These quality pieces of handwear contain extra knuckle and finger padding, along with palm and finger suction fibres to ensure these are sporting gloves at their most gripping—as form-fitting as a three-piece

Savile Row suit. Plus, the patented wrist-rolling design will ensure you are always over the top of your pull shot as you control it with a perfectly timed caress to the boundary. How good is that?

Bradfield Gold Star Batting Helmet

With its eye-catching design from the most acclaimed milliners in France, you will look an absolute picture in the *Breton* Gold Star Batting Helmet. And not only will you be the epitome of style and class, you will also be fully safeguarded under its world famous Triple Protection Guarantee. *Tres bien.*

Firstly, full protection from the brunt of a cricket ball from every possible angle, tested to an impact speed of 200 mph (320km/hr). Secondly, protection from dehydration, with microscopic perspiration-reduction air holes that keep your head up to 37% cooler than any other helmet on the market. Thirdly, the special Visi-Clear™ grill uses state of the art laser technology to invisibly clear the air immediately in front of and to the side of your eyes. Not even the tiniest dust particle will inhibit your view of the ball.

Clear gaze. Cool head. Safe from any blow. That's the Bradfield Gold Star Batting Helmet Triple Protection Guarantee.

HCCC Premier Thigh Guard

Made from a NASA-designed super-plastic, the HCCC Premier Thigh Guard is a little gem. It doesn't just guard your thigh, it offers it a comprehensive security service. You need not fear upper leg bruises ever again.

For a limited time, upgrade to the HCCC Premier Thigh Guard—Notch-Maker Edition, which comes with built in LED Notch technology. In the 1980s and 1990s, Mark Waugh was forced to register each first class century by scratching a stick man into his thigh guard. In the twenty-first century, register your landmark innings with a single tap. A top drawer piece of cricketing equipment.

Protecteur de Pénis Champion's Box

Hello, what's this then?

It's a customised box that fits precisely to your unique manhood. The *Protecteur de Pénis* Champion's Box app (available for both iOS and Android) will guide you step-by-step through the photographs required of your nether regions, ensuring both appropriate lighting and that all necessary angles and degrees of flaccidity are covered.

Once the full album of photos is entered into the app, it will automatically encrypt the images to prevent the kind of social media mishaps so easily made by some of my commentary box colleagues and send them securely to the *Protecteur de Pénis* Champion's Box data server. There, precision 3D printer technology will manufacture the perfect protector for your needs, complete with ultra-hardened exterior and sensual padded perfumed interior. This is the modern way of doing things. This is such exciting technology.

And it's such a pleasure to wear that you may forget you even have protection down there. Right up until the moment you need it.

ESCB Cement Elite Shoulder Cricket Bag

The exquisite ESCB Cement Elite Shoulder Cricket Bag exploits recent mathematical breakthroughs in fractal hypergeometry to create more interior space than the surface area would traditionally be capable of holding. Now you can comfortably fit all your cricket gear into the bag, with plenty of space remaining for other useful items such as sunscreen, spare underwear and diet pills (sold separately) .

The ESCB Cement Elite Shoulder Cricket Bag itself is a sublime piece of design, made from the purest hide of free range canvas llamas from southern Italy. With a 1500 thread count, it is such a delight to hold and touch that the rest of your body will envy your shoulder.

Such an elegant piece of technological sophistication and sexy design deserves to be treated with the utmost care. For this reason, the ESCB Cement Elite Shoulder Cricket Bag comes with a specially designed silk protector case, treated to be fully resistant to excessive heat, rain, mud, snow, alcohol and over thirty other different kinds of potential damaging environments.

That is fantastic. Really, really good. Take a bow, ESCB Cement.

● ● ●

Each individual piece of equipment listed here is world-class, the equipment equivalent of Malcolm Denzil Marshall or any of the other 1980s West Indian champion cricketers with whom I had the immense pleasure of playing during my county career.

But taken together, The Mark Nicholas Cricketer Kit—Deluxe Version is vastly more than the sum of its parts. It's one of the all-time greats, the kit equivalent of a 1980s West Indian cricket team.

It is genuinely the epitome of cricket kittery. A kit that almost defies belief. Magnificent stuff.

Masking the Darkness

AN EXCERPT FROM 'AUSTRALIAN PSYCHO: THE CAPTAIN'S DIARY'

One of the most controversial captain's diaries ever released, this book was deemed so disturbing it was only sold shrink-wrapped, a fate previously restricted to Len Pascoe's autobiography.

I check the time on my A. Lange and Söhne Zeitwerk Decimal Strike precision timepiece and note that it's still 47 minutes until the luncheon interval. If the unskilled catering staff has paid any attention at all to the instruction booklet I had FedExed over to them yesterday—and there will be hell to pay if it hasn't—they'll be preparing the shredded Brussels sprout and ricotta toast right now so they'll still have time for the caviar and crème fraîche tartlets later.

I'm pondering a declaration, something I find myself contemplating more and more these days. As I gaze through the window at the scoreboard, I sense the Channel Nine television cameras on me and the inevitable chatter of the commentators speculating on when I'll be making the decision, with millions upon millions of viewers listening to their guesswork, as if they have the faintest inkling whatsoever as to what is going through my mind. I glance up at the television monitor in the room and catch a glimpse of myself in the centre of the screen. Jesus, you should see how ripped my stomach is. The definition. Totally buffed.

My training regime is precise, totally eschewing the pitiful excuses of sleeping, dining or socialising to which weaker-willed individuals so desperately cling. A dozen sets of toning and strengthening exercises (40 reps) every morning and evening (stomach crunches, preacher curls, push-ups, side crunches, the cobra, burpees, split-squats, hamstring curls, reverse lunges, hovering presses and arm-breakers). I calculate if we win this Test early enough, I can get a 45 min Barre session in at the home gymnasium before the GQ photographer arrives for this evening's shoot. That's the American GQ, by the way. None of this GQ Australia bullshit.

Who's out in the middle now? It looks like Michael Hussey, with generic brand sunscreen splotched over his nose like some kind of primitive war paint, batting with George Bailey, who apparently still believes his ubiquitous smile can mask the darkness that so obviously lurks within.

"Hey, Skip," comes the baritone voice of one of the fast bowlers. I can *smell* him approaching, his retail antiperspirant barely repelling the onslaught of his body odour. I turn up the adjustable noise cancellation on my Bose QuietControl 30 wireless headphones with lightweight neckband design and allow myself to be transported elsewhere by the sublime pop of Huey Lewis and the News' 1983 smash hit single, 'If This Is It'.

The unshaven mesomorph inexplicably fails to comprehend my body language, or how much I'm enjoying Huey's impeccably catchy ode to the importance of communication in relationships and the termination thereof, and taps my shoulder. I somehow resist the urge to recoil from his touch as he asks me when we'll be declaring.

I ignore him and again turn my gaze out to the middle. Now I see that it's actually Shaun Marsh out there. And Ed Cowan. Or perhaps Chris Rogers. Who can say.

"We will declare the innings, Ryan, when I'm ready to do so and not a second sooner," I tell him, measuring each word precisely in order to ensure the conversation is ended with this single sentence.

He mumbles something about not being Ryan, but I'm already heading over to the refrigerator, where I retrieve my EHP Labs OxyShred Guava Paradise water. It's been kept precisely chilled throughout the innings to maximise hyper-lipolysis. I slug it down, feeling the metabolism-kickstarting burst of energy ripple right down to my Calvin Klein Men's Steel Micro boxer briefs.

I slam the empty bottle down. Hot damn. My guns are exquisite. I glance back out to the middle.

Shit. What are they doing out there? I specifically told David and Mitchell to accelerate the scoring. I also have the launch party for Hugh's new bar after my shoot tonight so I don't have time to waste with their defensive strokes. If we don't have enough runs to declare now, we won't win until just before stumps, and then I'll have to stay with the team into the early evening, which means I'll barely have enough time for my exfoliation regime before we leave for Hugh's.

I return to the fridge for my Blue Hill Bay Pastrami Smoked Salmon. I need some Omega-3 to calm me down. That's when one of the all-rounders—I want to say Marcus—tells me he threw it out because he thought it smelled 'off'.

I decide that's enough. If I have to spend another three quarters of an hour in a confined space with my colleagues, I'll wind up murdering them all with an axe.

I hold up my impeccably manicured hand and wave in Usman and Shane. I steal another glance at the television as I do so. My hair looks fantastic.

Head in the Clouds

**AN EXCERPT FROM 'PERRY-FECTION,
THE AUTOBIOGRAPHY OF ELLYSE PERRY'**

*The cricket hero's autobiography outperformed all expectations,
winning more awards and selling more copies than anybody
had predicted. Typical of her, really.*

My high school years were relatively uneventful. I was lucky enough to make the Pymble Ladies College soccer team (or 'kickball', as Mrs Farquar insisted we call it) at my first try-out, and was made captain. I remember thinking that was a little odd, but perhaps Mrs F felt sorry for me because I was the only Year Seven student in the team.

I also had the good fortune to make the PLC First XI cricket side. Coincidentally, I was made captain of that side, too, as well as the opening batsman and bowler. I happened to find some good form that first year and managed to score the most runs. Hardly surprising, since I was first one to the crease each time! As it turned out, I also topped the batting averages. And also the bowling averages. And took the most wickets overall. And catches. I must say, everything really seemed to click that year. And also in the rest of my school years too.

Yes, I led the athletics team and was named the school sports captain.

But I barely contributed to the PLC swimming team, anchoring only a couple of relays in the state finals each year. And although I broke the school cross-country record several years in a row, I think that was only because I kept miscalculating the distance I was supposed to run. I can be such a dunderhead sometimes.

Away from sports, I enjoyed my time in the school band. Although not so much the day at the Opera House when Mr Long fell ill just moments before we were due to perform Rachmaninoff's Symphony No. 2 in E Minor. Thank goodness I'd been so nervous during rehearsals that I'd watched him super-closely and was able to step in and conduct the orchestra. Disappointingly, however, I got distracted during my clarinet solo and as a result brought in the third violins a quarter-beat late during the final movement. Despite my sloppiness, the judges still kindly awarded us first place in the School Band Festival.

I decided to give the school band a miss after that (although I still regularly performed at school dances as part of my ska band 'El-Pez and the Dispensers'). But the School Spirit Award I'd been given for being in the right place at the right time to apply first aid and stabilise Mr Long after his heart attack had re-ignited my interest in school politics.

I'd long been captain of the political cartooning team at the school, ever since I'd edited the school paper and exposed Principal Kennington's kickbacks from the school fundraiser chocolate sales. I got a lot of credit for that scoop, but, if anything, I was angry with myself that I'd taken so long to unravel his misdemeanours. I had, after all, sold more chocolates than anybody else, thanks mostly to the lucky break of the lessons picked up when I portrayed master salesman Ricky Roma in 'Always Be Dancing', our school musical version of 'Glengarry Glenn Ross'. (A role I'd been given, I'm sure, solely because I'd been the only one foolish enough to write a faithful adaptation of the classic David Mamet play minus the profanity and with the addition of toe-tapping original songs.)

But my point is that if anybody should have known how the chocolate sales proceeds broke down, it was me. I guess I had my head in the clouds, arithmetic-wise, as I fretted about the upcoming International Mathematical Olympiad. Unnecessarily, as it turned out. My academic prowess had always been above average, although probably only because I'd been blessed enough to study several hours each night. Still, the gold medal was a nice keepsake.

Once I was made school captain, I was determined not to spread myself so thin again. Did the chess club really need another grand master? Couldn't somebody else run our award-winning Clean Up Australia Day campaign? (I still remember how furious I'd been with myself when I'd almost put my apple core in one of the recycling bins. The campaign deserved a leader more switched on than that.) Did I really want to give Solar Car Club another try after the previous year when they'd accused me of using a perpetual motion machine? (I had, in fact, merely developed a small nuclear fusion engine, which I maintain should have been allowed given that's precisely how the sun generates its energy.)

No. This time I would just focus on leading the school, keeping my grades up, reading to the elderly, designing the new school canteen, babysitting underprivileged children, judo practice, volunteering at the puppy shelter, maintaining the school intranet, my magic shows, the search for extra-terrestrial intelligence and representing Australia in cricket and kickball.

Infinite Improbability Drive

AN EXCERPT FROM 'THE HITCHHIKER'S GUIDE TO GLENN MAXI' BY PAUL 'FROGLESS' ADAMS

Here's a beloved passage from the science fiction classic written by the Proteas spinner once dubbed "the frog in the blender".

There is a theory which states that if ever anyone discovers exactly what Glenn Maxwell is for and why he is here, he will instantly disappear and be replaced by someone even more bizarre and inexplicable.

There is another theory which states that this has already happened.

Mickey Arthur pulled his electronic copy of The Hitchhiker's Guide to Glenn Maxi out of his satchel and looked at it again. The words 'DON'T PANIC' were printed on the cover in large, friendly letters. It was the only helpful or intelligible thing anybody had said to him throughout this entire tour of India.

Previously, Arthur had only read snippets of the book, but now he was determined to start from the beginning. Anything to avoid the phone call he was supposed to make.

Here's what that wholly remarkable book 'The Hitchhiker's Guide to Glenn Maxi' had to say about Glenn Maxwell.

"The Glenn Maxwell show," it says, "is big. Really big. You just won't believe how vastly, hugely, mind-bogglingly big it is. I mean, you may think it's entertaining to occasionally reverse-sweep an off-spinner to third man, but that's just peanuts to Glenn Maxwell. Listen…" and so on.

After a while, the style settles down a bit and it begins to tell you things you really need to know about Glenn Maxwell.

Like the art of taking flying catches over the boundary rope—in which the knack is in learning how to throw yourself at the ground and miss.

Or Isaac Asimov's Three Laws of Maxwellics.

1. Glenn Maxwell may not bore a human being or, through inaction, allow a human being to succumb to tedium.

2. Glenn Maxwell must obey the constraints of physics except where such constraints would conflict with the First Law.

3. Glenn Maxwell must protect his own wicket as long as such protection does not conflict with the First or Second Law.

Or the fact that famous science fiction author Arthur C. Clarke once posited the hypothesis that any sufficiently advanced Glenn Maxwell innings is indistinguishable from magic.

Arthur read all this with a blend of intrigue, delight and understanding before eventually realising that he was, in fact, reading it with the exact opposite blend of boredom, horror and confusion. Startled by this realisation, Arthur hid the guide away in the hotel closet. He had no time to read about Glenn Maxwell now, anyway.

Arthur had already told three of the four players who'd failed to complete their homework that they'd been suspended. Now he wanted to relax, have a bath and maybe a strong cup of tea. But before he could, he had one more player to call.

Arthur took a deep breath and dialled the number.

"I think you ought to know I'm feeling very depressed," was how the player answered the phone.

Arthur sighed. "Well, we hardly want to gain comic mileage from any form of mental illness," he said. "Not in this day and age."

"No," came the morose reply.

"We're generally more sophisticated and sensitive about those kinds of things than we were in the 1970s," said Arthur. He flipped through his phone and texted through the number of the team psychiatrist.

There was a long pause. "I'm not getting you down at all, am I?" asked the player.

"No, not at all," said Arthur.

"I wouldn't like to think I was getting you down."

"No," said Arthur. "That's quite all right. I just wanted to discuss with you the homework."

"I remember," he sighed. "Here I am, cricket mind the size of a planet and you ask me to do homework."

"Yes, yes," said Arthur. "But the problem is that all we got from you was an SMS that read '42'. That's not even an answer to a question we asked."

"I suppose it isn't," said the player.

"And you see," continued Arthur. "By *not* doing your homework after I'd threatened to suspend anybody who didn't do their homework, I'm now left with what even the most poorly trained of logicians would be forced to conclude is very little choice but to suspend you."

"I see."

"For not doing your homework," said Arthur.

"Yes."

There was another long pause. "If it's any consolation it's just for the one game of cricket," said Arthur eventually.

"Cricket," said the player. "Don't talk to me about cricket."

"Just be grateful we're not making you listen to Vogesian poetry," said

Arthur. He again urged him to call the team psychiatrist and hung up.

Arthur sighed. Finally, a chance to relax. He found his towel, fished the Hitchhiker's Guide to Glenn Maxi out of the closet and started running the bath.

As he settled in, he began to read about the extraordinary details of Glenn Maxwell's latest shot, the infinite improbability drive, which the guide describes as 'a wonderful new method of reaching the boundary in a split-second; without all that tedious mucking about in the infield. As the improbability drive reaches infinite improbability, it passes through every conceivable point in every conceivable cricket ground almost simultaneously.'

Arthur smiled. Just thinking about the shot gave him the very strong feeling he'd now gotten through the worst of it.

Which was why it was such a shame that just three months later, mere days before the Ashes was about to commence, Arthur's Australian coaching world was destroyed to make way for a Darren Lehmann bypass.

Popular Landmarks for the Ashes Holiday Bucket List

AN EXCERPT FROM 'THE BARMY ARMY GUIDE TO VISITING AUSTRALIA

Regular tourism guides weren't particularly useful for cricket fanatics, or even those who just liked to drink enormous amounts of alcohol. That's why the Barmy Army started releasing its own travel books for members.

You've travelled more than 10,000 miles to the other side of the planet for the Ashes. Obviously, your number one priority is to drink heavily and sing loudly in the vicinity of the cricket for the next several weeks.

But if you ever get a free day in the schedule you may find yourself curious about some of the world-famous tourist attractions Australia has to offer.

We've summarised some of the major ones here.

Great Barrier Reef

The Great Barrier Reef is the world's largest coral reef system, stretching along the coast of Queensland on the north-eastern side of Australia. Much like the career of Alastair Cook, it's considered one of the Natural Wonders of the World.

ARMY CHECKLIST

Likelihood of horrific sunburn: High

Tolerance for incessant drunken singing: Low—sadly, fewer than fifteen percent of Barmy Army members can sing while snorkelling.

Alcohol availability: Medium

Recommendation: *Avoid.* The series is yet to begin. Hopes for an England victory are at their highest. Why run the risk of being eaten by a shark and ruining everything?

For other things to do while waiting for the series to start, check out Chapter Two: 'What To Do When A Person Inexplicably Shouts 'Queenslander' At You And Other First Test Problems'.

Barossa Valley

The Barossa Valley is a major wine-producing region of South Australia, not far from Adelaide Oval. Its vineyards provide some of the finest Shiraz wines in the world.

ARMY CHECKLIST

Likelihood of horrific sunburn: Medium

Tolerance for incessant drunken singing: Medium

Alcohol availability: High

Recommendation: *Avoid.* Having just visited the site of the 2006-07 Adelaide Test—still cruelly dubbed 'Amazing Adelaide' by insensitive locals—patriotic Englishmen will find themselves stirred by strong emotions. Better to stick together during this tough time. Find a pub.

Other things to do in Adelaide while you wait for the Second Test to start can be found in Chapter Three: 'I Guess Maybe We Can Have A Look At A Church Or Something?'

Rottnest Island

Rottnest Island is a small island off the coast of Perth. It's the natural habitat of quokkas, the small, rare native marsupials.

ARMY CHECKLIST

Likelihood of horrific sunburn: Medium

Tolerance for incessant drunken singing: Low

Alcohol availability: Low

Recommendation: *Avoid*. Why on Earth would you want to confront a small, hairy Australian beast in its natural habitat? Didn't we get enough of that throughout Ricky Ponting's career?

Other things to do in Perth can be found in Chapter Four: 'The Bar Where Jonny Bairstow Allegedly Got His Headbutt On And Other Places To Get Shitfaced During The Third Test.'

Great Ocean Road

The Great Ocean Road is a 150-mile stretch of road along the southern coast of Australia. It provides beautiful views of limestone rock formations standing proudly in the sea.

ARMY CHECKLIST

Likelihood of horrific sunburn: Low

Tolerance for incessant drunken singing: High

Alcohol availability: None

Recommendation: *Avoid*. It's the Christmas season! Why would you stop drinking long enough to get behind the wheel of a car? If you want to experience a spectacular drive, then you should instead be watching Joe Root as he powers one through the covers.

For more information on other tourist attractions in the vicinity of Melbourne, widely considered the cultural capital of Australia, check out Chapter Five: 'The Ramsay Street Bus Tour and Other Australian Culture You'll Be Too Drunk To Investigate During The Fourth Test.'

Sydney Opera House

The Sydney Opera House is one of the most famous buildings in the world, with distinctive shell-tiled sails and a prime location looking over Sydney Harbour.

ARMY CHECKLIST

Likelihood of horrific sunburn: Low

Tolerance for incessant drunken singing: Low

Alcohol availability: High

Recommendation: *Avoid*. Almost none of the performances that take place in the Opera House are cricket-based. It's mostly classical orchestras and opera and shit. But check if *Shane Warne: The Musical* is playing. It won't be, but just in case.

For more information on other famous Sydney landmarks, including the Sydney Harbour Bridge, Bondi Beach and the apartment of Mark Nicholas, see Chapter Six: 'Irish Pubs and Other Drinking Venues To Attend During The Fifth Test.'

The Truth Behind Allegations of Spot-Fixing-Fixing

THE EPILOGUE TO 'SEE SPOT-FIXING RUN, AN INTRODUCTION TO THE FUN, EXCITEMENT AND CRIMINAL UNDERBELLY OF SPOT-FIXING'

The definitive book on spot-fixing contains a chilling epilogue that changed many people's perceptions about how gambling messes with their enjoyment of cricket.

Spot-fixing, like cricket, never stands still. As more and more allegations of spot-fixing in cricket appear around the world, many betting syndicates have taken to wagering on the details of these allegations of spot-fixing.

A wide variety of exotic bets is available for these allegations of spot-fixing. For example, gamblers can choose to bet in which paragraph an explanation of spot-fixing will be placed. Bets can also be taken on whether a simplified example of 'how spot-fixing works' will be included within the piece itself (and, if so, in which paragraph) or as a separate article, guaranteeing the publisher more clicks.

In most articles, these explanations or examples take place early on, often in the first or second paragraph, and the odds offered by the bookies will reflect that. However, some journalists will instead choose to place their breakdown of the basics of spot-fixing later in the piece, in an attempt to grab the reader's attention early with a flashy opening paragraph. Wise gamblers will look at the form of the journalist in question, and attempt to predict their stylistic flourishes.

The betting syndicates also offer markets on which nations will be implicated in the allegations, and how many players from each of those nations will be alleged to be involved. Gamblers keen to attract big winnings can also bet on whether or not any specific players will be named—this is, of course, exceedingly rare.

There are also the over/under bets, where a benchmark sentence is given and the gambler must then choose whether the first allegation will be made before or after that sentence.

For example, if the over/under sentence is 10.5, and the first allegation of spot-fixing is made in any of the first ten sentences of the piece, then anybody who bet on 'under' would win.

Again, sensible gamblers will investigate the style of the journalist in question. Some writers go into their pieces with a very high sentence-rate and will often burn through sentences in a single word, or sometimes two before even considering making their allegations.

Risky. Very risky.

These are just some of the simpler bets that can be placed on allegations of spot-fixing. But more sophisticated options are available for veteran gamblers looking to add an extra layer of excitement. Will infinitives be carelessly split? What will be the longest string of redundant, unnecessary, superfluous adjectives? How many concepts in the piece will be phrased in the form of a question? There is a market for everything.

Needless to say, as the betting market on allegations of spot-fixing has matured, many journalists have been approached to 'fix' their writing about the allegations. And unfortunately for some, the temptation has proven too hard to resist.

To many cricket writing fans, this seems difficult to believe. Why would these wealthy journalists, some of whom probably earn millions for a single stint doing ball-by-ball blogs for the IPL, risk everything to fix their piece on allegations of spot-fixing?

Sadly, the 'rock star' lifestyle of the modern cricket writer isn't enough for many of these individuals. Being rewarded handsomely for one's ability to write about people hitting a cricket ball may look like a dream come true for cricket-writing fans around the world. But the free time, hotel lifestyle and enormous incomes can so often lure talented cricket writers into an insidious world of hard partying, hard drinking and podcasting.

Once they've trodden this path, the corrupted cricket writers have left themselves open to illegal betting syndicates blackmailing them into doing their bidding. And that's where the opportunity to fix an allegation of spot-fixing arises.

While this is tragic for the writer involved, the fact remains that the fixing of allegations of spot-fixing is a blight on the coverage of this great game. Readers need to know that writing about allegations of spot-fixing is untainted by corruption.

Sadly, this is clearly not the case. My most recent investigations have uncovered several scribes who have taken money from bookies to fix their pieces alleging match-fixing. There is even audio tape of one senior cricket correspondent agreeing to end a sentence in the fourth paragraph of his expose with a preposition, a grammatical misstep that is clearly visible in the final piece. The passive voice was also used an improbably high number of times by another cricket writer in his piece, precisely as predicted by the informer.

For legal reasons, the identities of those cricket writers will not be revealed here. But rest assured, their details have been passed on to the relevant authorities.

Bets Paid Out—
Allegations of 'Allegations of Fixing' Fixing

DETAILS OF BET	RESULT	ODDS
Nations named	NONE	1.90
Number of writers implicated	SEVERAL	8.50
Writers named?	NO	1.05
First explanation of 'Allegations of Spot-Fixing' Fixing	PARAGRAPH 2	1.60
Number of 'meta' jokes in which piece refers to a literary concept while exhibiting that concept itself	5+	1.20
Comical analogy implying cricket writers lead similar lifestyle to the cricketers they cover	YES	1.85
Piece becomes so convoluted it disappears up its own backside	YES	1.01

Wicked Maidens

AN EXCERPT FROM 'WHAT THE LEG-SPINNER SAW' BY ANONYMOUS

Heavily censored by Cricket Australia upon its initial publication, here for the first time is an example of the unexpurgated version of the underground classic, whose author remains unknown.

The first ball of the over was tossed outside off stump, harmlessly turning away and into the keeper's gloves.

"I'll loosen you up," the masseuse, Tiffany, had promised after yesterday's play. She possessed wavy blonde hair, full pouting lips and honours diplomas in many different styles of massage.

After a long day in the field, he was very stiff. But Tiffany worked on him for close to three hours. Her fingers probed and pressed—sometimes gentle, but more often not. Her sublime touch was exactly what he needed and he gratefully submitted to her precise caress. Any muscle that needed attention, Tiffany found. She then massaged it over and over and over until the ache was released.

Finally, just when he thought he was done, she found other body parts that elicited fresh moans from him. Moans that inevitably led to further activity.

Afterwards, more relaxed than he'd felt in a long time, he headed to the hotel.

The second ball was a wrong'un. It drifted away from the batsman, who played outside the line as it turned sharply back.

Back in his hotel room he'd been surprised to find three women—Annabelle, Gillian and Emily—who were waiting for him and described themselves as his biggest fans. Annabelle was strawberry blonde, with sultry eyes and a curiously straight nose. Gillian, the redhead, had the smoothest skin he'd ever seen, like some kind of sexy tree frog. And Emily, the youngest of the trio, was a brazen brunette with a low-cut top that barely restrained her perfectly spherical breasts.

"How did you get in here?" he asked. "What do you want?"

"Can I have your autograph?" asked Emily, straightening her posture to reveal a marker pen held firmly within her décolletage.

"I want to see your googly," purred Annabelle.

"Would we be able to sleep over?" asked Gillian, her eyes wide with pleading.

He couldn't bear to disappoint such devoted fans, so immediately went to work fulfilling all their requests.

Several hours later, however, none of them had managed any sleep. And the prospect of this state of affairs changing seemed more and more remote. The girls were more insatiable fans of his than he'd imagined.

The batsman advanced to the third ball but was beaten in flight. Alas, the keeper fumbled the chance and the batsman made it safely back to his crease. A lucky escape.

He'd eventually escaped from the room around 3am while the jacuzzi was heating up and made his way to the concierge's desk. As a professional, he needed to find some way to get a few hours' sleep before the day's play.

The concierge, Kirsty, was a raven-haired beauty with high cheekbones and symmetrical eyebrows. Her body had been poured into her uniform like Crown Lager into a World Cup trophy. "Is it possible for me to be given another room, please?" he asked.

"I'm afraid the hotel is completely full, sir," she said. She looked from side to side, then confidentially leaned over the desk to him. The buttons of her blouse strained against her bountiful, enhanced breasts. "But I'm sure I can find a bed for you," she whispered.

Kirsty walked out from behind the desk and strode confidently down the hall. He struggled to tear his gaze away from her, and she turned back to face him.

"Come with me," she said, breathily.

He decided to do so. Sleep would have to be further delayed.

He tossed up his fourth ball. Again, no run as mid-on safely fielded a confident drive.

His cab driver this morning had been Bryana, a golden-haired waif who drove like she looked—dangerous and with no regard for society's conventions.

Spending the remainder of the night in a different room had caused him to miss the team bus, which meant he needed to make his own way to the ground. It was only as the taxi arrived there that he realised his wallet was still back in his hotel room.

Bryana pulled into an alley and locked the doors. "You'll have to find some other way to work off your debt then," she said. "Why should I give you a free ride?"

He grasped what she was saying. "You deserve to be fully compensated," he said. "With a generous tip," he added.

"Oh, I want more than the tip," replied Bryana, undoing her seatbelt and climbing into the back seat.

The fifth ball was flatter, faster.
The batsman went to cut it, but was too late.

Now very late, he'd raced into the ground. He was stopped by Khloe at the gate. Tall, strong and blonde, she was all woman and, more relevantly, all security guard.

"You can't get to the dressing room from this gate," she said, putting her hand to his chest to stop him from going further.

"I need to get in," he said.

"I know that," she said, with a sly smirk. Khloe ran her hand down his chest and torso and beyond, before eventually stopping. "But from here, it's very hard."

Her hand moved some more. "This is the Members' End," she said. "Do you understand what I'm telling you?"

He nodded.

Khloe took him aside and a full body inspection was conducted. Eventually, he was allowed to enter.

Once through, he had no time to do anything other than sprint straight onto the ground and begin bowling.

The final ball of the over was a classic leg break.
It spun again past the outside edge of the bat.

The over complete, he returned to the boundary edge and applause from the crowd. In particular, a blonde bounced in approval, licked her lips and gave him an enigmatic stare as he approached.

He gave a small wave back at her. Acknowledgement of yet another maiden in his spell.

Except, as he took his fielding position, he suddenly realised to his horror that this was no maiden. This was his wife.

He gulped.

Freeway of Finality

**AN EXCERPT FROM 'THE AUTOBAHN OF AUTOBIOGRAPHIES'
BY DAMIEN 'THE BOWLOLOGIST' FLEMING**

Damien 'The Bowlologist' Fleming played 20 Tests and 88 ODIs for Australia without once using that nickname. In his autobiography he compares and contrasts the final overs of the two World Cup semi-finals he played.

Coming in to bowl the final over of the 1999 World Cup semi-final against South Africa, I felt like I'd gone through the Doorway of Déjà vu.

South Africa needed nine runs to win with their most dangerous batsman, Lance Klusener—The Slogologist—on strike. They had one wicket remaining.

Three years earlier, I'd also bowled the final over of the 1996 World Cup semi-final, against the West Indies. On that occasion, it had been the Wide-Brimmed Hatologist, Richie Richardson, on strike, needing ten runs to win with two wickets in hand.

I had surely entered the Sunroom of Similarity, but, truth be told, the Pathway of Parallels had begun well before the final over.

In both games, we'd batted first and stumbled into the Cafeteria of Collapses. In 1996 we'd been 4/15. In 1999, it wasn't quite as bad, but at 4/68, it wasn't particularly great either.

On both occasions, it was Michael Bevan—The Finishologist—who led the recovery. In 1996 with Stuart Law. In 1999 with Steve Waugh.

In 1996 we recovered to 8/207 off our 50 overs. In 1999 it was 213 all out from 49.2. These were reasonable scores given the poor starts but both targets were still very much in the Boulevard of Below-Par Batting.

In 1996, the West Indies got off to a solid start, so the captain threw the ball to Shane Warne—the Gyno... [Editorial note: Damien Fleming had not yet thought up a nickname for Warne at this point]—who took a wicket with his first ball. West Indies 1/25 off 6.1 overs.

In 1999, with South Africa off to an even better start, the captain threw the ball to Warne, who took a wicket with his second ball. South Africa was 1/48 off 12.2 overs.

From there the oppositions' innings became less similar. To paraphrase The Poetryologist, Robert Frost: *"Two Roadways of Run-Chases diverged in a canary-yellow Wood of Wicket-Taking..."*

In 1996 the West Indies took the Pathway of Prosperity, cruising untroubled to 2/165. From there they needed just 42 runs from 53 balls to win, with eight wickets in hand.

But when I took a Catch of Calamity-Inducement to get rid of Chanderpaul for 80, the West Indies were 3/165. From there they lost regular wickets in a Flash-Flood of Foolishness. Suddenly they were 4/173 (Harper out for 2), 5/178 (Gibson, 1), 6/183 (Adams, 2), 7/187 (Arthurton, 0) and 8/194 (Bishop, 3).

In 1999 South Africa instead went down the Cul-de-sac of Conservative Consolidation. From 4/61 from 21.2 overs they cautiously recovered to 4/145. But at that point they needed 69 runs from 57 balls to win. And their attempts to attend the Auditorium of Acceleration resulted in the fall of wickets. Only Klusener's arrival at the crease saw them close the gap, even as wickets fell at the other end.

The two 'chasing' innings had diverged in the middle but now we'd reached the final over in each semi-final. And as I took the ball and entered the Abattoir of Anxiety, I couldn't help but feel the Sluice of Sameness wash over me.

In 1996 Richardson hit my first ball for four.

In 1999 Klusener did the same.

In both semi-finals I had officially begun worshipping at the Shrine of Shitting Myself.

In 1996 the second ball of my over saw Richardson attempt a Single of Senselessness, only for Curtly Ambrose to be run out by an underarm throw from the Gloveologist, Ian Healy. I then bowled Courtney Walsh with the third ball of the over to give us victory. We had taken 8/37 to win the match.

In 1999 the second ball of my over went less well. Klusener clubbed that one for another four and the scores were now level. From the third ball, with the field in, Allan Donald backed up too far and was almost run out by the Boofologist, Darren Lehmann.

And then the fourth ball...

Klusener mistimed it to mid-off, where Mark Waugh gathered and flicked the ball back to me. By this stage Klusener had completed the match-winning run. Unfortunately for South Africa, Donald had yet to begin.

As Donald took off, I rolled the ball to Adam Gilchrist—the Walkologist—at the other end, not realising it would trigger my own journey to the Mausoleum of Madness.

Prior to that delivery I would have described the ball as 'rolling down the pitch for a possible victory'.

But now, with its travel seeming to take an eternity, my mind snapped. After what felt like a millennia watching it, the ball was now instead on an Avenue of Ascendancy, a Pathway of Pre-Eminence, a Turnpike of Triumph, a Carriageway of Conquest, an Overpass of Overpowering and so on and so on and so on.

Gilchrist gathered the ball ten thousand years later, completed the run out and we went through to face Pakistan in the final, which we won comfortably.

Yes, I had lost my mind. But it was a small sacrifice to win a World Cup. And I've long since learned to live with the condition that the Psychologologist would later diagnose as Chronic Alliterative Metaphoritis.

Or, as I prefer to call it, my Whirligig of Wordplay Weirdness.

Averages, Geometry and Combinatorics - the Quiz

AN EXCERPT FROM 'MATHEMATICS FOR UNDER-14 CRICKETERS'

Can you correctly answer the questions in this quiz from the world's leading cricket-based mathematics textbook?

QUESTION 1

Sir Donald Bradman scored 6,996 runs and was dismissed 70 times for a final Test batting average of 99.94. Assume that The Don was reanimated using dark magic and recalled as a zombie number three batsman for Australia.

a) If he made ducks in the first ten innings of his undead recall, what would his batting average now be?

b) Now calculate his batting average if the following ten innings of the next Test series *also* saw him dismissed without scoring each time.

c) How many consecutive ducks would Zombie Bradman need to be dismissed for in total before his Test average dropped below 60?

d) Below 50?

e) At what point does this become ridiculous?

QUESTION 2

In the final PowerPlay of an ODI, five fielders are allowed on the boundary.

a) Using only compasses and straight edge, construct a regular pentagon inside a circle to represent an optimally placed set of outfielders for the death overs.

b) Hence, or otherwise, prove that Glenn Maxwell will reverse-sweep the bowler for six. Show your working.

QUESTION 3

There are six Sheffield Shield teams in Australia, each with six specialist batsmen. Assume the Australian selectors are looking to pick a top six for the national side.

a) Prove that there are 1,947,792 possible top six combinations the selectors can come up with.

b) Explain to the Australian public why the eventual side chosen must necessarily contain Shaun Marsh.

QUESTION 4

Pat Cummins is attempting to york Kane Williamson. Assume that Cummins releases the ball from 2.5m above the ground towards the feet of Kane Williamson, 20m away.

a) Construct a right-angled triangle with Cummins and his outstretched arm as one side and the length of the pitch another side. Use the Pythagoras Rule to calculate the length of the hypotenuse and, hence, how far the ball must travel.

b) Assume Cummins is bowling at 150km/h. Determine how long it will take for the yorker to reach Williamson's feet.

c) If Kane Williamson is 1.73m tall, determine how long it would take for the ball to instead reach Williamson's head.

d) Derive a beamer function that shows how tempting that reduction in reaction time would be to Cummins if Williamson had somehow brilliantly got underneath the previous attempted yorker and swatted the ball over the cover boundary for six.

QUESTION 5

The Venn diagram below shows the manner in which South Africa has previously exited World Cup tournaments. Use your understanding of Venn diagrams and South African heartbreak to correctly place the following future World Cup scenarios onto the diagram.

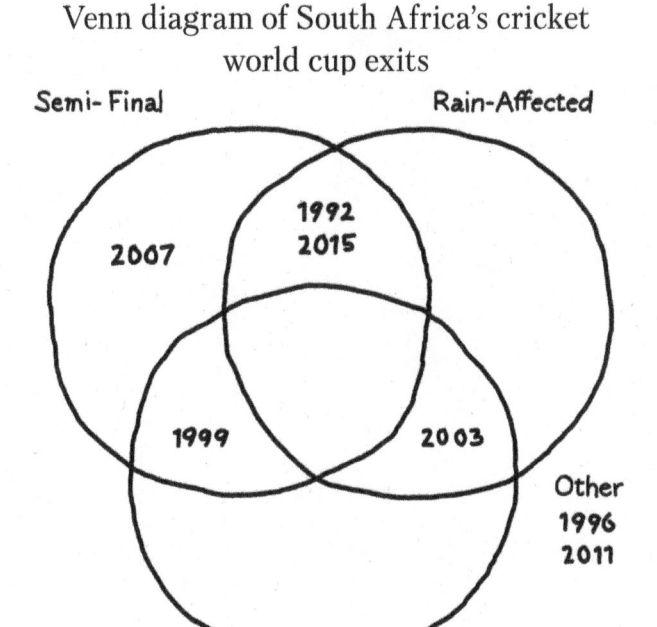

Venn diagram of South Africa's cricket world cup exits

Semi-Final

Rain-Affected

2007

1992
2015

1999

2003

Other
1996
2011

Tie

a) With South Africa needing just seven runs to win the second semi-final with four wickets in hand and fourteen overs remaining, Joe Root brings himself on to bowl and takes 4/6 in his first over to end the match. (Assume that England have a better net run rate than South Africa.)

b) Batting first, South Africa make 481 all out from 49.3 overs in their final must-win Super Six game. After a brief shower during the break and an inexplicable DLS computer glitch, Bangladesh are set 34 from 49 overs, which they achieve with 47 overs to spare.

c). With scores level in the semi-final against India, a flash flood prevents South Africa's final batsman from leaving the dressing room. He is timed out and at the insistence of Indian television rights holders, Virat Kohli's men qualify for the final.

d) A lion eats Quinton de Kock.

The Modern Game

**AN EXCERPT FROM 'ON THE BRIGHT SIDE—
A POSITIVE VIEW OF CRICKET'
BY NEIL HARVEY**

*A member of Bradman's Invincibles,
Harvey always revels in what's
great about the modern game*

I like big bats.

Furthermore, I cannot lie, I like everything they bring to the modern game. In my day, you'd get an outside edge, and it would go straight through to the keeper and you'd be out. A rubbish aspect of cricket.

Not these days. These days, the outside edge is like another face of the bat, and I think that's just swell. If you get an outside edge, it's more likely to go for six than to be caught behind. This prevents fielders from lollygagging about and keeps them on their toes. Literally so, if they're reaching to stop those sixes. Just one of the many reasons you need a tall drink of water like Big Billy Stanlake on the boundary.

Big bats literally make for a more multi-dimensional batting experience. Why bat in two dimensions—with just the face of the bat—when you can bat in three or, in the case of Glenn Maxwell, somehow even more?

I am yet to see evidence that Maxwell understands—or is constrained by—the concept of space-time as we know it.

Maxwell is my kind of batsman. Sure, in the 1940s and '50s you needed to mind your p's and q's at the crease. Keep a straight bat and a solid defence and no monkey business. In today's cricketing world, however, monkey business seems to be the key to the entire thing. You can't compile an acceptable innings in the modern game without playing the kind of shots that, in my day, would have seen you immediately dropped from the side and shipped off to the circus.

Nobody does modern monkey business batting better than that rapscallion Maxwell. My goodness, I don't even know the names of all the shots he plays. Sometimes he'll play a cover drive. I'll recognise those. But otherwise, I don't have the foggiest idea what he's doing. It's possible that he doesn't either. And that makes for splendid viewing.

Would Maxwell have been a success in the Invincibles? You bet your britches he would. Conversely, what would Bradman have achieved in an IPL tournament? Diddly-squat, I suggest. Not that any other batsman from my era would have done any better. The modern cricketer is just that much more skillful and exciting than the namby-pamby nit-wits we had in my day.

And nowhere are modern cricketers more skillful or exciting to watch than in the field. Some people say that I was a fine fielder when I played, but the fielding know-how of players today makes me look like a bumbling clown. That business where they skedaddle around the boundary rope, jump over it and, lickety-split, throw it back to another fielder? That's fine entertainment. It's like seeing a juggling troupe busking on the outskirts of a cricket match. Sure, it can be a bit of a dog-and-pony show. But if they left their cap there, I'd toss in a couple of bucks as a thank you, let me tell you.

Thank goodness we switched from fences to ropes too, or we'd never see any of this. I particularly enjoy when the umpire doesn't know if the fielder has stopped the ball before they've gone over the rope and we get to see the television umpire dilly-dally through sometimes dozens of replays to confirm whether the batsman has scored four or just three. The sight of a cricketer sliding frame-by-frame into a rope lets you experience the thrill of modern fielding that much more. Why, if I had my druthers, I'd spend most of the entire day's play in front of the idiot box watching a young man—or, more and more often these days, a young woman!—sliding into a rope. I never used to think that about fences.

If you think it's just the marvellous fielding that batsmen have to worry about these days, then you've got another think coming. Because that's just poppycock. Modern bowlers are the bee's knees too. Have you seen these 'slower balls' that are all the rage with today's young fast bowlers? Do you think Frank Tyson ever had the wherewithal to bowl a slower ball? No. Tyson just kept on trying to bowl faster and faster and faster. Utterly pig-headed was Typhoon. The thought of going in the other direction simply never crossed his mind.

But it crosses the minds of modern bowlers all the time. Why, I've seen A.J. Tye bowl six slower balls in an over. Flabbergasting stuff. In my day, that was considered just medium pace bowling and you'd cart that joker all around the ground. Not these days. These days, you need to have your wits about you as a batsman to deal with all the bowlers' shenanigans.

By the way, I think it's jim-dandy when they call batsmen 'batters' these days. Batter sounds so much better. It reminds me of getting fish and chips from the corner store as a young lad growing up in Fitzroy. Does the word 'batsman' trigger that kind of nostalgia? Not at all. But 'batter' does, and that's yet another reason why modern cricket is so much better than in my day. Why, in my entire Test career, I don't think I ever once reminisced about getting fish and chips. But I think about it all the time these days. If I recall correctly, it used to cost me tuppence for a couple of pieces of whiting and a large serve of chips. Sometimes you'd even get a couple of potato cakes as well.

Yes. Potato *cakes*. If any of you sick mongrels call them potato scallops, I will bloody well fight you.

Jedis, Jokers & The Don

AN EXCERPT FROM 'MIKE HUSSEY'S GUIDE TO THE MOVIES'

What are the best movies of all time? Mr Cricket's book promises to tell you.

Star Wars Episode IV: A New Hope (1977)

A young farm boy from a desert planet joins forces with a mysterious Jedi Master, a pair of droids, a cocky pilot and his enormous bear-like co-pilot to rescue a princess from the evil Galactic Empire. Despite a running time of 121 minutes, the movie contains *no* cricket. ★★

The Dark Knight (2008)

A terrifying criminal mastermind is determined to wreak chaos on Gotham City and only The Dark Knight can put an end to his criminal reign. The joke, however, is on us, because despite an almost constant stream of bat references, not a single one turns out to be made of English willow. ★

Se7en (1995)

A pair of detectives attempt to track down a serial killer who is gruesomely murdering his innocent victims. Alas, at no point in the film does a scurried three become a seven thanks to four overthrows. The seven in the title instead refers to the number of deadly sins or something. ★

The Godfather (1972)

A mob patriarch is determined to keep his favourite son out of the family business, but circumstances conspire to make this impossible. Annoyingly, despite regular references to The Don, Test cricket's greatest ever batsman fails to make an appearance. ★★

Shaun of the Dead (2004)

A zom-rom-com, where a man's attempts to win back his girlfriend are threatened by the sudden phenomenon of the dead rising from the grave. In one excellent scene—easily one of the very best in modern cinema—the titular Shaun (Simon Pegg) wields a cricket bat. Sadly, rather than select a team of the living to challenge a makeshift Zombie XI to, say, a best-of-five ODI series, he instead clobbers them in the head. ★★★★

Pinocchio (1940)

A puppet is determined to become a real boy in this Disney animated 'classic'. The promise of cricket being an integral part of this movie again proves grossly misleading, however, when the only sign of it turns out to be some form of know-it-all do-gooder cartoon insect. Makes you so mad you just want to smash a stump into Pinocchio's face. Unnecessarily, because somebody already appears to have beaten you to it. ★

Being The Best

AN EXCERPT FROM 'WHITE CAP, BLACK CAP, GETTING THINGS DONE THE PROPER, NEW ZEALAND WAY' BY BRENDON MCCULLUM

After retiring from international cricket, the Kiwi legend released a self-help book on how to conduct one's life in the proper, New Zealand way. Records indicate he also donated all profits to charity. Because of course he did.

When I was New Zealand cricket captain, people used to ask me all the time why our team had such strong moral fibre compared to other nations. I was never quite sure what the answer was. To be honest, I never really thought it was my place to say we were ethically superior to other teams. My job, as I saw it, was instead to use that moral high ground to teach other cricketing nations how to better themselves. To reach down, offer them a little bit of Kiwi wisdom and moral certainty and help them ascend to our plane.

Sure, that might seem impossible, but it *can* be done. After all, many of the other players in my team didn't start off as the superhumanly virtuous citizens of cricket that you see these days. I had to show them how to go about it.

For example, there were many times early on when I'd have to go have a chat with Trent Boult after a day's play and get him to reflect on what he was doing. How did he think knocking over international batsmen—

some of them considered among the very best in their country—made *them* feel? Did he ever stop to think that they were probably completely embarrassed by how foolish he'd made them look? Yes, other countries do it to us, but that doesn't mean we should stoop to their level.

I also remember when Kane Williamson scored a double century against Sri Lanka. I was absolutely furious with him and let him know in no uncertain terms how disappointed I was with his antics. Sri Lanka were guests in our country and here Kane was, showing off by making not just one century against them, but two. In one innings! And he would have probably made a third if I hadn't declared the innings closed. Utterly childish. I promise you he's a better man than what he put on display that day.

But they're the challenges you have to deal with as a captain. I would drill into my players over and over that it wasn't whether we won or lost that was important. It was how we played the game. Could we walk off the field at the end of the day, proud of how we'd behaved?

Often I had no idea what the match score was. I preferred it that way and used to tell ground staff to find me a dressing room where it was impossible to see the scoreboard. Usually they'd say they didn't have such a dressing room available and so I'd offer to instead go sit in the back of one of the food outlets while my teammates batted. Sometimes, during the busier times of day, I'd help out the catering staff, putting on another serve of chippies or refilling the bottles of tomato sauce or whatnot.

When we were out in the field, some of my teammates would occasionally slip up and give me a clue as to what the score was but I'd always shush them before they gave too much away.

The only score I was keeping track of was the balance we'd achieved between doing things the right way and doing things the wrong way. And, on this front, I was determined to keep the wrong way to nil. I'm pleased to say that we achieved this much more often than not.

In contrast, have a look at the way Australia plays. For example, look at all the World Cups they've won and ask yourself: is that really necessary? Is winning really that important to them? Is that why they play the game?

Now, I don't want to have a go at Australian cricketers. Most of them are lovely blokes and I won't hear a word said against them.

Yes, sometimes they go too far in their pursuit of victory. Sometimes they'll say things I think they probably regret once they've cooled down a bit. Sometimes they'll sledge when it's not necessary. Or there'll be a bit of niggle. Or incessant abuse. Or swear words that aren't really called for.

And, yes, sometimes they'll claim a catch that didn't carry. Or not walk when they've clearly edged it. Or throw the ball a little too close to the batsman than is probably needed. Or rough up a ball with sandpaper. Or bowl the ball underarm. Or knock the bails off with their hand and appeal. Or push every single playing condition and Law of the game to the absolute bloody limit (and perhaps slightly beyond) at every possible moment just so they have a marginally improved chance of winning a game of cricket.

But apart from little lapses like that, they're champion blokes one and all. Yes, they sometimes say and do things they later regret. But then, who in international cricket doesn't?

Oh, that's right. Us.

Because we're New Goddamn Zealand, the nicest and fairest team to ever play international cricket.

Handled The Ball

AN EXCERPT FROM 'OUT! THE HISTORY OF CRICKET'S MODES OF DISMISSAL' BY JARROD KIMBER

Kimber is a writer for ESPNCricinfo. In 2018, while serving six months in prison, he wrote a book on the history of cricket's forms of dismissal.

Steve Waugh stands at the crease, squinting from beneath his helmet as Harbhajan Singh approaches the crease. It's 2001 and Waugh is a mythical warrior-king whose legendary mental strength is discussed in whispered awe.

Waugh looks up as Harbhajan bowls. He is approaching from over the wicket, the ball is flighted in to the pads. Judging the length, Waugh plays his favourite shot—the slog-sweep—but misses and is hit on the pads. The men around the bat burst into appeal. Harbhajan joins in, despite the ball clearly angling down leg side. But just as the last echoes of their shout die on their collective vocal cords, they are suddenly renewed.

For the ball has spun off Waugh's pads, above the batsman's head and is now bouncing towards the stumps. In that instant Waugh loses his superhuman mind and parries the ball away with his hand.

Steve Waugh is out handled the ball.

● ● ●

Handled the ball is a dismissal from a Monty Python sketch. 'How were you out, eh? Nudge, nudge. How were you *dismissed*?' 'Handled the ball'. 'Ooh, I bet you did, I bet you did. Handled the ball, eh, squire? Say no more.'

It's a form of dismissal too lewd to be awarded to the bowler. And unlike a run out, which, in modern times, is generally credited to at least one fielder, the salacious nature of a handled the ball wicket sees it cast adrift from the fielding side. It is a scorecard orphan, claimed by nobody. A piece of raunchy filth that can be blamed solely on the disgusting, onanistic urges of a batsman who couldn't control himself.

Nudge, nudge. Wink, wink.

Say no more. Except ...

● ● ●

It is 1979. Pakistan is in Australia, 1-0 up in a two Test series.

It is a Pakistan team that, like all Pakistan teams, is equally willing to battle itself as its opponents. Pakistan was the *Suicide Squad* movie before *Suicide Squad* even existed. Just with a much better Rotten Tomatoes score.

Its inner conflict is just one of the many aspects that makes Pakistan such an exquisite cricket team. It is all of us, a blend of inner demons wrestling with one another in a failed attempt to present an acceptable face to the outside world.

Javed Miandad is part of this team. On the next tour he will captain Pakistan and be kicked at by Dennis Lillee.

Imran Khan is part of this team. In 1992 he will captain Pakistan, fight like tigers and win a World Cup.

Sarfraz Nawaz is part of this team. On this tour he has already invented reverse swing and taken 9/86 at the MCG, including an X-rated spell of 7/1 that wins the First Test.

Sarfraz does not take seven wickets with this next ball. Nor does he concede one run. Instead Ric Darling drives uppishly to mid-off where the ball is safely fielded. The mid-off fielder lobs the ball back to the bowler's end where non-striker Andrew Hilditch picks it up and gently tosses it back to the bowler.

But Sarfraz isn't catching the ball. Instead he is turning to the umpire and appealing.

Andrew Hilditch is out handled the ball.

● ● ●

There have been ten handled the ball dismissals in the history of international cricket. Apart from Waugh and Hilditch, the others to succumb to handling the ball were Russell Endean (South Africa), Mohsin Khan (Pakistan), Desmond Haynes (West Indies), Mohinder Amarnath (India), Graham Gooch (England), Daryl Cullinan (South Africa), Michael Vaughan (England) and Chamu Chibhabha (Zimbabwe).

Ten handled the ball victims in almost 150 years of cricket.

There will be no more.

● ● ●

Ben Stokes is facing Mitchell Starc. It is 2015. England has regained the Ashes in a Test series both one-sided (the margins of victory were 169 runs, 405 runs, eight wickets, an innings and 78 runs, and an innings and 46 runs) and, in the end, close (the eventual series result was 3-2). The one-day series is not yet so paradoxical.

It is the second ODI of the series and Starc bowls a fuller ball to Stokes, who defends it back to the bowler. Starc realises that the batsman has lost his balance in the process of jamming down on the yorker. With Stokes out of his crease, Starc throws the ball back at the stumps. Stokes recoils and, in the process, hurls out his hand to deflect the ball.

Social media erupts. Half those watching call Stokes' reaction instinctive. The other half deem it wilful. These halves are, unsurprisingly, split almost wholly by national allegiance.

The third umpire has no national allegiance. He reads Stokes' mind and determines his reaction to have been wilful.

Ben Stokes is not out handled the ball.

Ben Stokes is out obstructing the field.

● ● ●

The movie *Wall Street* is most famous for the scene in which Gordon Gekko, played by Michael Douglas, decrees that 'greed is good'. Like many of the most beloved movie quotes, such as 'Play it again, Sam' or 'Dude, where's my car?', this is a misquote. The 'greed is good' phrase was not delivered as part of Douglas' Oscar-winning performance. At least, not in that form. The full quote from Gekko is 'greed, for lack of a better word, is good'.

The in-sentence clarification serves its purpose in the quote. Sometimes a better word *is* lacking.

But cricket did not lack a better word for handled the ball. The handled the ball dismissal was perfectly described. There was a ball and the batsman handled it.

And yet, in 2017, obstructing the field swallowed it whole, in an ICC-backed hostile takeover that would have served *Wall Street* proud.

Words matter.

Concepts matter.

Handled the ball matters.

● ● ●

Before the unholy merger between handled the ball and obstructing the field, T20 number-crunchers began research into the potential of obstructing the field dismissals.

Anybody with a passing interest in probability theory knows the perils of small sample sizes. But cricket's finest sabermetricians and statisticians were working their way past those pitfalls, using bold numerical techniques and algorithms to open up a new foothold against batsmen.

It is an important area to probe. Mitchell Starc had proved against Ben Stokes that an obstructing the field dismissal could be instigated by the fielding side. As a result, obstructing the field had suddenly become a form of dismissal open to further optimisation.

In January 2018, during the seventh season of the Big Bash League, Alex Ross was given out obstructing the field. The analysis and planning had begun to bear rare fruit, despite the difficulties that had been posed by the ICC's ill-considered merger.

Handled the ball is not obstructing the field. The fielding side cannot instigate a handled the ball wicket. It is a mental error. Obstructing the field is a physical error. And it can be instigated by fielders. To conflate the two is not wrong because it's an historical affront but because it's a fundamental taxonomical error.

Ultimately, it's a minor challenge for the statisticians. The number-crunchers will stat their way past the hurdle of these two forms of dismissal being merged. They will determine which of the new obstructing the field dismissals were physically instigated and which were a mental lapse. They will note the distinction in their databases. They will conduct their analyses in accordance with those notes.

But the scorecard will no longer reflect the distinction. A piece of history will be lost to the rest of us.

Because handled the ball is out.

Expanded Cricket Roles

**AN EXCERPT FROM 'WHITHER CRICKET?,
ESSAYS AND MUSINGS ON THE FUTURE OF THE GAME'**

*Is Test cricket dead? No. It's just stunned, if this thrilling vision
of the future of the game is to be believed.*

For too long, cricket has been dominated by players fulfilling the traditional boring roles of batsman, bowler and wicketkeeper.

The modern game, however, is so much more than just batting, bowling and fielding. It's time to expand. Here are some new roles that teams should adopt.

Press Spinner

One of the best things about Test cricket is that, by virtue of the fact it takes place over multiple days, press conferences can be used as a strategic weapon in the game.

Currently, the role of spinning press conferences in order to attack the morale and psyche of the opposition is very much a part-time role. It shouldn't stay that way. There's plenty of scope to select a specialist press-spinner, who can turn small doubts on wearing minds into big psychological stumpers.

Cricket is at least ninety percent a mental game. And it's a game that's covered by vast numbers of media outlets. Time to select a player who can exploit these twin facts and spin his team to victory.

Wicketkeeper-Statsman

Many years ago, it was considered enough for wicketkeepers to be good with the gloves, taking catches, pulling off stumpings, whispering sledges into the ears of batsmen.

Then came the rise of the wicketkeeper-batsman, where an ability to contribute significantly with the bat became a fundamental part of the role.

Now, however, the position needs to evolve again. The most important role a wicketkeeper needs to play in the modern game is that of helping the captain decide on DRS reviews. Currently, this is done by gut instinct. But the role needs to move beyond that.

A proper wicketkeeper-statsman would have studied the basics of probability theory and understand the nuances of Bayes Theorem. Using this, they could correctly combine the likelihood of the umpire making a mistake with the probability of the particular delivery evading umpire's call and delivering an out verdict, weighted by expected future runs that the batsman might score. With all these factors taken into consideration, they could make the optimal decision of whether or not to review. Maximising DRS success rates in a mathematically sound fashion would almost certainly be worth more than a few big hits coming in at number seven.

Seem Bowler

As mentioned above, DRS has changed the game. Fielding teams won't just stop with wicketkeeper-statsmen, whose main focus is a defensive one, trying to prevent the misuse of his side's reviews.

The logical next step in optimising DRS reviews is to go on the offence.

Don't just protect your reviews. Actively try to get the batsmen to waste theirs. Crucial to this strategy will be the 'seem bowler', who will take wickets in ways that *seem* to be unjustified. The seem bowler's deliveries will seem to pitch outside leg. Or seem to be bouncing too high. Or seem to be striking the pad outside the line of off stump.

Whatever it takes to get the batsmen to waste their reviews in trying to overturn the umpiring decisions. It's one thing to deceive one batsman and dismiss him LBW. It's quite another to also deceive the non-striker into agreeing to review the decision. Only the most accurate of seem bowlers need apply.

Social Boundary Rider

Sledging, or 'mental disintegration', as Steve Waugh lovingly euphemised it, is a regular tactic for many sides. But when does a bit of banter designed to upset a batsman's concentration go too far and cross the line into abuse? How do teams stay up to date with ever-changing standards of community etiquette and social conduct? Or navigate the expectations of what's a fair verbal target and what's beyond the pale in different cultures and countries? In other words, how do you make a cricket team 'woke'?

Enter the social boundary rider, a specialist who roams the outskirts of societal norms, ensuring that sledges and taunts are kept within the boundaries, so that Virat Kohli never unfriends you on Facebook.

First Dropped

Even with the new roles proposed here, teams will still lose games. And, inevitably, scapegoats will be called for by the media, general public and loudmouth Twitter trolls.

This can be frustrating, especially when the eleven originally chosen was thought to be the best team the selectors could have picked. Yielding to the call for the axe and dropping any member of the best possible side chosen would inevitably weaken the team.

The solution? Pre-select a player to be first dropped. In the event of a defeat, this player would then be the one to make way, satisfying the bloodlust of fans, while simultaneously working to make the team stronger. That's the kind of foresight and professionalism modern cricket so desperately needs.

Calling It In

THE INTRODUCTION TO 'THE VOGES CONSPIRACY'

A true crime classic. Go behind the scenes to examine how a conspiracy of cricket statisticians tried to remove Adam Voges from the record books.

March 2, 2018

The Association of Cricket Statisticians and Historians runs on a budget of less than twenty million dollars per year. Despite this, they monitor cricket statistics, records and feats for international and first class games all around the world and provide a vital point of contact for cricket statistics emergencies.

Naturally, they were the first people that Kristy called.

Listening back to the recording of that phone call, knowing everything we know now, is bone-chilling.

"ACS," says Ashleigh[1], the young woman in the unfortunate position of answering Kristy's call. Initially there's a rote professionalism to her voice. "How can I help you?"

"He's gone," screams Kristy. She's clearly distraught, barely able to get the words out.

---

1 Several of the names in this book have been changed by request

"Who's gone?" asks Ashleigh.

"Adam," says Kristy, the syllables almost lost under her sobs. "Adam's gone."

"Adam who?" asks Ashleigh. It seems like a foolish question now, of course. But that's only because we have the cruel benefit of hindsight. At the time, there was no reason that Ashleigh would have known. There's no reason *anybody* would have known.

Kristy can't answer her. All you can hear on the recording is her weeping.

"I'm sorry, ma'am," tries Ashleigh again. "But if you want me to help you, you'll have to provide more information. Why don't we start with your name?"

"Kr— Kristy," she says, the words a struggle to bring together.

"Hi, Kristy," says Ashleigh. "Thank you for calling ACS. My name's Ashleigh and I'm here to help you. Can you please tell me again why you're calling?"

Kristy audibly pulls herself together, taking several long breaths, before continuing. "It's Adam," she says, as calmly as she can. "He's gone. The others are all there. Bradman, Smudge, Pollock, Headley, Sutcliffe, Weekes. Even Sobers. But Adam… is gone." And whatever composure she was able to muster disappears beneath fresh wailing.

And now on the recording you can hear Ashleigh's training kick in as she begins to piece together the clues she's been given. "Adam *Voges*?" she says. You can hear the tell-tale taps of a computer keyboard as Ashleigh searches for more information. "Is this… is this Kristy Voges?"

"Yes," says Kristy, the word choked out.

"And are you saying…" There's a telling pause here, as if Ashleigh dare not even ask the question. "That Adam is no longer being shown on a list of top Test batting averages?"

"Yes."

And then, pandemonium.

● ● ●

This is where our story begins. A single phone call from a distraught wife that would put ACS investigators on the trail of a global numerical crime. An investigation that would eventually unravel the greatest cricketing statistical conspiracy since the Australia v The Rest of the World 2005 ICC Super Series was given official status.

Wizened Detective Ric Finlay would lead the investigation. Finlay was a veteran statistical investigator, a man who knew numbers backwards as well as forwards, but not even he was prepared for the devious plot he was about to discover.

The clues from that initial Test match broadcast of a Voges-less table that had so upset Kristy would lead Finlay all around the world.

To the West Indies to visit the grave of Andy Ganteaume, the man with a better average than Bradman, albeit from only one Test.

To Western Australia to talk with Shaun Marsh, the man who shared a 449-run partnership with Adam Voges in an innings that single-knockedly added 11 runs to Voges' final batting average.

Over to Hobart, the site of that partnership, to investigate the conditions at Bellerive Oval and also get a change of clothes at his home, just a short drive away.

To ACS headquarters itself, to explore why their acronym lacks an H despite clearly being designated an Association of Cricket Statisticians and *Historians*.

Then back to the West Indies to look into the demise of a once-great cricketing superpower and how their modern day impotence provided the motive to undermine Voges' Test batting records.

Throughout these tax deductible journeys, Finlay inched ever closer to a rogue group of statisticians, working behind the scenes to change the cut-off for Test batting averages from 20 innings to 1500 runs, solely to ensure that Adam Voges disappeared from the most acclaimed cricket table of them all.

This much of the story is now well-known, of course, thanks primarily to the work of Finlay and his team.

But Finlay discovered something far darker. Something that threatened to unravel our very understanding of the worth of a batsman, and the methods by which we measure it.

This is the story of that investigation.

A Serpent's Lament

AN EXCERPT FROM 'THE INESSENTIAL NEVILLE CARDUS'

One of the lost essays from the inimitable Neville Cardus, recently discovered during the auction of Alec Stewart's prized collection of Beano comics.

August 1953

I cannot believe that summer is on the wane. But the evidence of the calendar is beyond dispute and it is now time to reflect on the lessons learnt in the course of recent months' events.

No doubt I shall court folly if I fail to mention the visit by the Australian cricket team and the manner in which their robust supporters highlighted a significant failing among the followers of English cricket. The Australians, as ever, go into action full of life, missing nothing and taking the measure of everything. This was clearly seen in their raucous adoption of the 'beer snake', the best crowd innovation since the war.

For those dull fellows not initiated in this fine invention, the 'beer snake' is fabricated from the empty plastic cups in which ales are served at various watering holes around the ground. The size and shape of these vessels are such that they agglomerate in as flush a manner as possible. This is evidently a manufacturing choice taken in response to inarguably strong forces of commerce, and a design whose chief intention is to ease the transportation and storage of the containers.

However, as the cup's life cycle accedes to the looming spectre of its inevitable end, and having served its primary function of holding a beverage for the duration of its consumption, its potent stackability becomes the key to the anatomy of the 'beer snake'. For this trait now permits those crowd members participating in the serpentine ritual to simply 'stack' their empty cups, one atop the other.

Although these items are unimpressive when gathered in small numbers, the visual effect rapidly approaches a 'critical mass' at approximately twenty cups. Beyond that threshold, what was merely a stack of plastic cups transforms into a swaying, reticulated, snakelike organism. Furthermore, with careful co-ordination, several smaller 'beer snakes' can be assembled in disparate areas of the stand, then met and combined into larger and larger serpents. En masse, the resultant hybrid is stately, without being pompous.

The scheming for the creature's construction invariably takes place in utmost secrecy, for scurrilous ground officials have chosen to exhibit relentless enmity towards the 'beer snake'. To their eternal shame, I say. Dame Resourcefulness doesn't often come to us with her gifts if first time we are fool enough not to accept them.

And yet the impact of such officious negativity serves only to breathe greater life into the fiction. Like the genuine serpent it emulates, the shy creature slowly gathers energy throughout the day, growing in secret beneath the seating, appearing only at day's end, held aloft in a stunning emergence from its burrow. Its transparent skin glistening in the fading English afternoon sunshine can't help but remind one of the glow of a dramatic soprano as she reaches for the upper notes in

Brünnhilde's opening war cry of *Die Walküre*; the end result is equally breathtaking.

After a languid summer of experimentation, the public's wish, nay thirst, for these pythonic structures brooks no argument; they have left the country agog.

The canny inventiveness of the Australian cricket fan leaves me in a state of mild despair. County cricket in the lump has not been so resourceful, and the underlying basis for this failing merits exploration. Is it the presence of so many lethal snakes in the Australians' homeland that sparks such enterprise? Or is it the sheer volume of beer they famously consume as a nation and the ensuant debris that gives them access to the raw materials required? I fancy that it is a synthesis of the two factors.

A very fierce letter appeared in the Press suggesting the 'beer snake' was foul, iniquitous and offensive to the taste of sportsmen. The horrible dust raised by the cheap Press on this topic is, in a word, graceless. They allowed vulgar journalism to come between their vision and the true deeds. The idea that any Antipodean development is inherently crass is a ruinous one.

A more relevant question is this: how has English cricket fallen so far behind its great rival? I fear that regaining the Ashes will be considered a hollow triumph unless we can swiftly rectify our performance in the court of lager-based serpentine construction.

Just as Saint Patrick drove the snakes from Ireland, has the licence to bring wine and champagne into Lord's driven 'beer snakes' from the Home of Cricket? While I have no desire to undervalue the inventiveness of the English, the nation that spawned the industrial revolution, it seems improbable that one can breathe life into a facsimile of any of God's great creatures using wine bottles.

To the critic with some eye for inborn style and culture, it might seem plausible that the bottles could be strapped together with the belt of one of the Members to create a representation of an octopus or other cephalopod. However, this is a venture perhaps best left for the most inebriated members of the cricket viewing public, whose drunken flights of fancy remain the steam engine that hauls the freight of crowd escapades beyond the perilous summit of boredom's peak. They shall match the Australians if they put their collective mind to it, of that I have no doubt.

However, it was not just the introduction of the 'beer snake' that saw Australian crowds so dominate the recently concluded series. They also brought with them the notion of the 'Mexican wave', in which members of the crowd take it in turns to stand up and then sit down again, waving merrily as they do so.

This is certainly an arena in which the great English public could easily be expected to surpass their southern hemisphere counterparts. For, at its heart, the 'Mexican wave' bears the essence of nothing more complicated than a queue. And I defy any other nation to exhibit the queueing prowess of the modern Briton, for whom a good style and an organised technique prevails in all circumstances. By the time the Australians tour next I would be disappointed and surprised were we not to demonstrate to them a degree of 'Mexican waving' that leaves them both impressed and severely daunted.

I fear, however, that the same cannot be said for the third aspect of the triad of crowd innovations introduced by the Australians over the past months. I refer, of course, to the notion of 'streaking'.

This is the least seemly of the three inspirations and one that I don't believe will 'catch on' here. The prospect of removing one's garments and transgressing onto the field of play simply does not often take it into an Englishman's head. Apologies to my Australian friends, some of whom I count among my closest and least capricious.

We shall 'take you on' in the arena of the 'beer snake', despite the limitations to which I referred above. We will surely dominate in the

'Mexican waving' with a rapidity that should come as no shock. But the inherent modesty of the average Englishman and the unflattering climate that surrounds him will leave 'streaking' as a crowd entertainment to be pursued solely by other nations of the Empire.

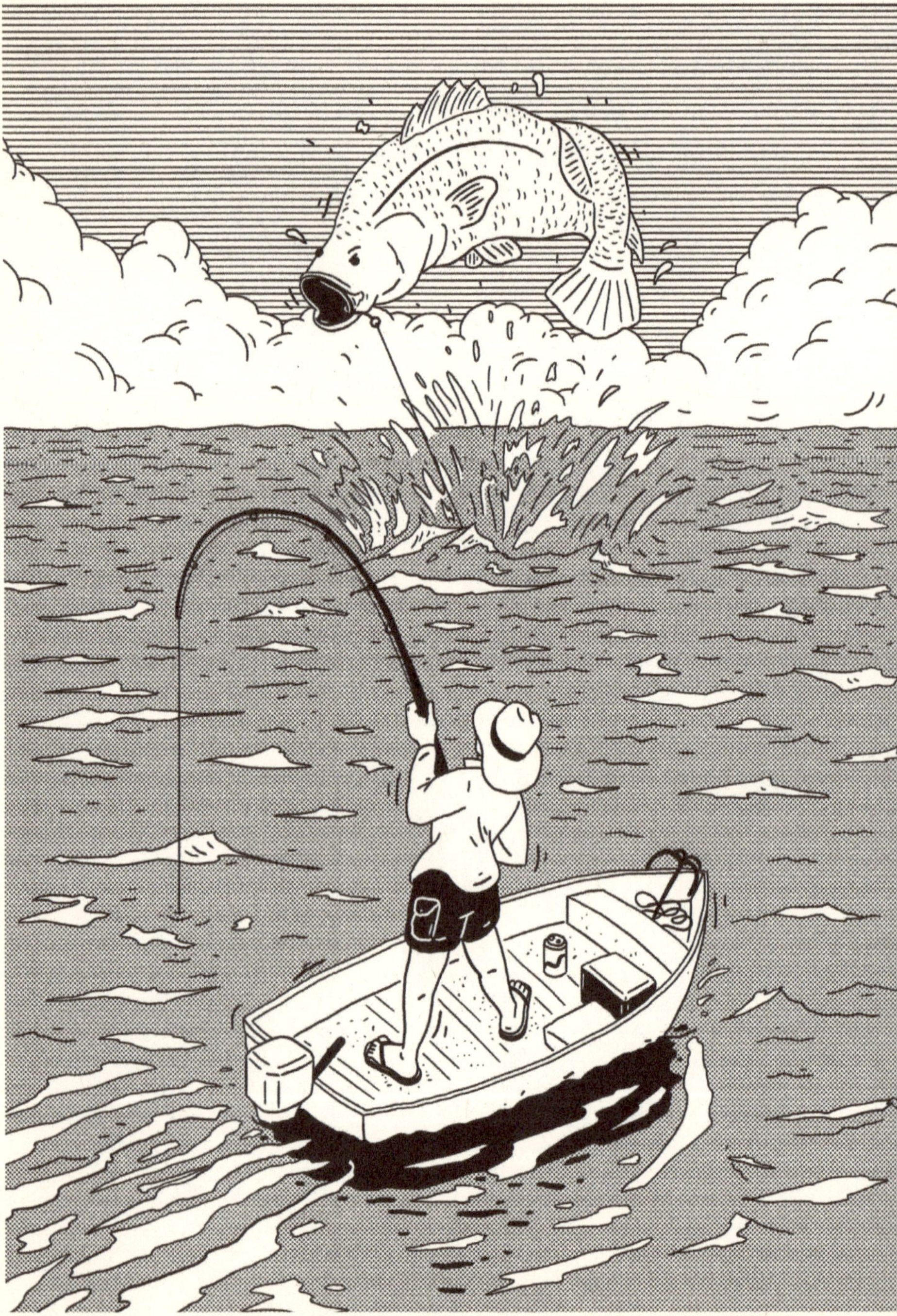

Waiting For a Return

AN EXCERPT FROM 'THE OLD MAN AND THE SEAM'
BY MATTHEW HAYDEN

Hayden's critically acclaimed debut novella is an allegorical commentary on his career as both a cricketer and a fisherman.

A wave crashed over Matthias. He woke with a start. His dreams had been as troubling and relentless as a Curtly Ambrose spell.

He had dreamt of the fishing village again. Of the children. The women. The other fishermen. Also, another child he didn't know, visiting from another village. Or perhaps a midget. He seemed to have a moustache.

They were all gathered at the dock. Watching for him.

The dream was true. He knew that. Maybe not the moustachioed midget. Maybe that was a visiting child after all. Or some kind of rock wallaby.

But the rest of it was as true as the Bellerive Oval deck.

The villagers were waiting for his return. Waiting for his failure.

He would never give them the satisfaction.

He unstrapped himself from the chair. He'd been dozing in it all night.

Now he needed to stretch his legs. To walk, like Adam Gilchrist in a World Cup semi-final.

There wasn't much fresh water left. Not after this many days at sea. And there was even less food. But he might be able to scrape together a meal. Sustain himself for another day.

But as he stood the weight on the end of his rod spoke to him in the fisherman's language.

Finally.

"Barramundi," it said.

Matthias smiled. A barramundi was the leg side full toss of fishing. Delicious. Enticing. And there was no feeling quite like when you hooked a big one.

He would not be returning to the village empty-handed, like a Phil Tufnell outfield chance. Not this time.

He'd show them all.

Matthias strapped himself back in.

He pulled on the rod. Felt the delicious resistance of the barra.

Time to work.

● ● ●

Through three days and nights Matthias fought the fish. He ached all over. But the pain was exquisite, like a Damien Martyn cover drive.

The heat of the noon sun each day had seen his skin redden and blister.

As the sun had set and the moon had risen, the clouds had come. And with them, the rain. Inevitable, like Kevin Mitchell Junior over-ruling the umpires and bringing on the covers.

The boat had pitched from side to side. Waves had crashed over him, indistinguishable from the storm.

The torrential water had washed away his remaining strength. And with it his sins.

He had strained for breath. For stamina. For a glimmer of hope.

He had never felt more beaten.

He had never felt more alive.

Now, as dawn broke yet again, the great fish summoned fresh energy. It thrashed away. Matthias gripped his rod. Held tight. He couldn't fight the barra's raw power. But he could wait it out.

This was surely its last surge.

It had to be.

● ● ●

As the morning sun continued to rise Matthias finally felt the barra's energy wane. It had fought the good fight. But now it was done.

The fish's epic struggle for freedom had earned his admiration, like a triple century record-breaking innings, even if some people said it was just against Zimbabwe.

But now its fight was over. All that was left was for him to finish it.

Matthias crossed himself and muttered the Lord's prayer.

He pulled. Hard, like Ricky Ponting to a ball pitched short of a length. And with an almighty heave, Matthias reeled the fish in. It landed in his arms, knocking him from his chair.

He collapsed on the deck, still holding the great barramundi.

For long minutes, he held his adversary close. Eventually, he rolled away from its embrace.

As he did, he pulled the hook from the fish's mouth. The barb jabbed into his hands. It tore at his flesh.

Total exhaustion gripped him, as if he'd made a century in fifty degree Sharjah heat and single-handedly outscored both of Pakistan's innings in reply.

He was spent.

"Roy," he called, unable to lift his head.

No answer.

Where was Roy? Was he even here? Or had he imagined it?

"Roy," he called again.

The barra flopped beside him.

Matthias looked into its eyes. It continued to flop like Mike Atherton facing up to Glenn McGrath. And, like Atherton against McGrath, it would soon be at its end.

"Brother," whispered Matthias. He tried to kiss his great foe. Not in a homosexual or weird way, but as a sign of respect.

But he could no longer move. His muscles refused to budge, like Steve Waugh being called through for a risky single.

After a few minutes, Matthias stopped trying. He would just be still. He'd won. That was all that mattered. He'd shown everybody.

He lay flat on the deck, arms stretched wide. A fish hook in each palm. Blood flowing freely, like runs at the Gabba.

All he could see now was the sun.

Bright. Warm. Comforting.

The light called to him like JL urging him through for a single to turn over the strike and put pressure back on the bowlers

"Mother," he whispered.

And closed his eyes.

● ● ●

BBQ Barramundi Recipe

INGREDIENTS

4 tbsp olive oil
5 x 250g pieces barramundi, skin on
assorted herbs
250g butter
3 lemons, juiced

METHOD

1. Catch a barramundi, ideally in a novella filled with powerful symbolism. Gut, scale, and cut into 250g pieces.

2. Heat a heavy frying pan on high. Add the oil to the pan.

3. Season the barra steaks with preferred herbs. Avoid obnoxious little weeds.

4. Place the barra steaks skin side down. Press down firmly to prevent skin curling and ensure crispiness.

5. As the fish cooks, relax the pressure, leaving it to cook. Do not turn.

6. After a few minutes, shake the pan. This will prevent the fish from sticking. When the flesh of the fish feels warm to the touch, flip it with a spatula and cook for thirty more seconds.

7. Remove the fish from the pan and place on a tray. Return the pan to the heat and add the butter.

8. Once the butter is caramel-brown, add the lemon juice and more herbs.

9. Serve immediately over the barra steaks. Offer to your mates.

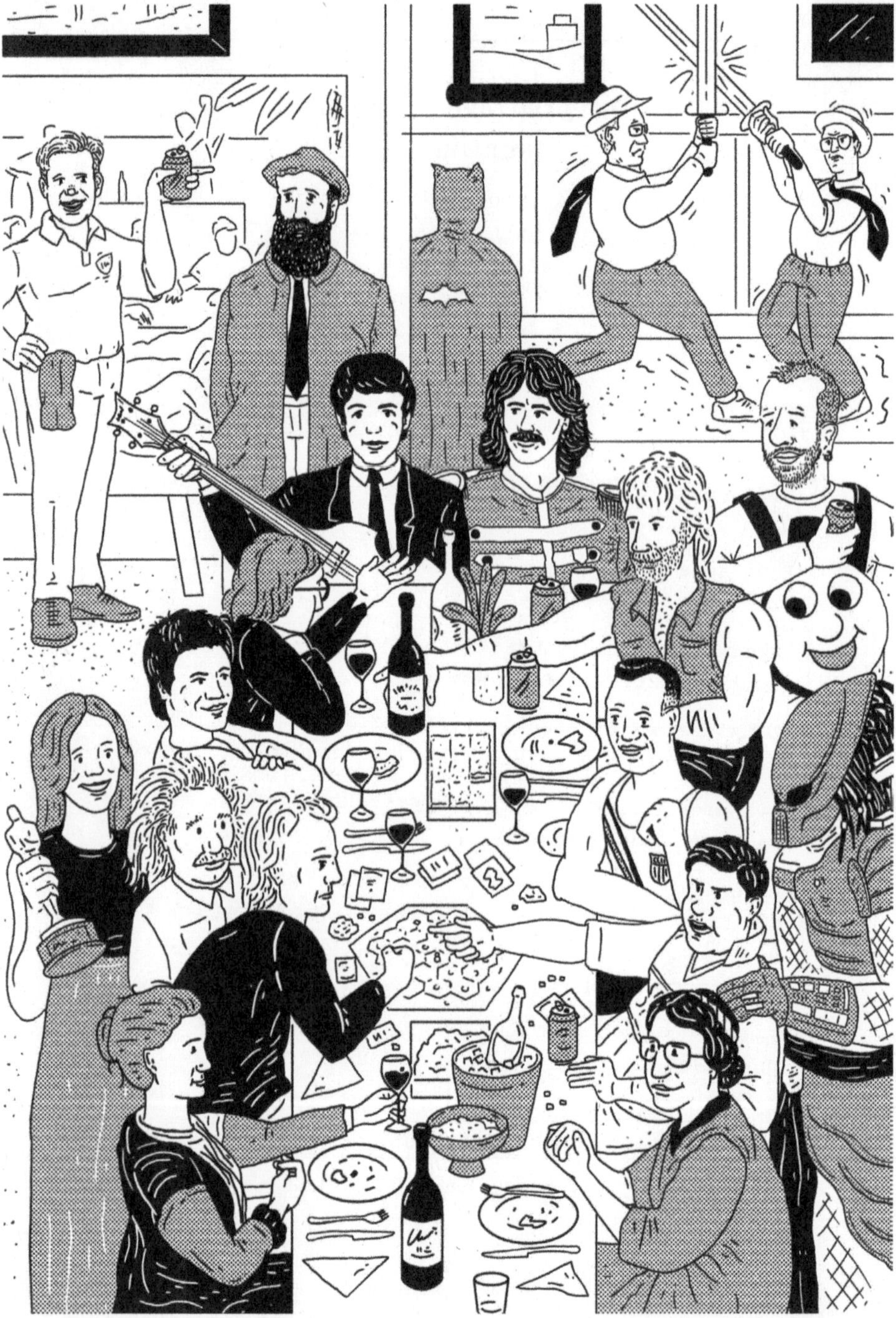

Astonishing True Secret No.41 - Murali's Mural

AN EXCERPT FROM 'ASTONISHING SECRETS OF INTERNATIONAL CRICKETERS: A GOOD MAIL SERIES'

With newspaper revenues declining, British tabloids have turned to releasing trade paperback compilations of their most sensational journalism. This piece received unprecedented numbers of reader comments online.

Long-Time Spinning Rivals Face Off Again in the World of Art!

The rivalry between champion Australian leg-spinner Shane Warne and Sri Lanka's off-spinning sensation Muttiah Muralitharan has flared again with revelations that Murali has unveiled a stunning painting designed to show up his long-time spinning rival.

It had long been known that Warne commissioned a mind-blowing mural of himself hosting a remarkable party of celebrities and friends, living and dead, including Marilyn Monroe and a topless Angelina Jolie. The mural, which also features JFK, Elvis Presley, and Jack Nicholson carrying a slab of VB, reportedly holds pride of place in Warne's study.

13% Bigger, Better and Crazier— Murali Triumphs Over Warne Once More!

But Murali, who famously tussled with Warne for the record of most Test wickets throughout their careers, reportedly trumped his leg-spinning adversary yet again with his astonishing work of art. Close pals of the Sri Lankan spin star who have seen Murali's magnificent mural say it's at least 13% bigger, better and crazier than Warne's.

Yum! Tamil Tweaker Tantalises Taste Buds!

Where Warne was seen hosting a barbecue by the pool in his picture, the Kandy-born spin hero's transcendent painting allegedly takes place at a sophisticated dinner party, where guests dine on traditional Sri Lankan cuisine such as Kiribath, Lunumiris and Toblerone.

All You Need Is Art! Is Murali the Fifth Beatle?

And although Frank Sinatra, Mick Jagger and Bruce Springsteen were guests at Warne's imaginary gathering, Murali's stylish soiree is said to have been attended by all four of the Beatles. Intriguingly, however, the record-holding Test wicket-taker has invited the Fab Four members from different eras of their spectacular careers. Paul McCartney has shown up from the mop top Beatlemania era. George Harrison appears, moustached, from the later Sgt Pepper period. John Lennon has popped in, bearded but Yoko-less, from his acclaimed post-Beatles solo career. And Ringo Starr has come dressed as Thomas the Tank Engine.

If It Bleeds, We Can Invite It To Our Party!

Boxing great Muhammad Ali was a guest at the party in Warne's mural. But close friends of Murali have claimed that his striking painting depicts even more impressive fighters, including Bruce Lee, Chuck Norris and a Predator from the popular film franchise of the same name.

The Sri Lankan Superstar Turns Heads the Other Way, Inviting Sophisticated and Successful Women to his Classy Dinner Party!

And whereas the female attendees of Warne's barbecue—Jolie, Monroe and Sharon Stone—were seemingly chosen primarily for their physical attributes, the women at Murali's dazzling dinner party are said to include inspirational figures such as Rosa Parks, Marie Curie and Academy Award-winning director for *The Hurt Locker*, Kathryn Bigelow. Only one of them is said to have shown up topless.

Catan's Not Going To Settle Itself! Doosra-Bowling Champion Knows How To Keep His Guests Entertained!

Several of Warne's guests, including James Dean, play poker by the side of the pool in the leg-spinner's painting. In contrast, Murali's guests—including Heath Ledger, Albert Einstein and former captain Arjuna Ranatunga—are enjoying a spirited game of Settlers of Catan. Arjuna has apparently called for a runner, who appears to be Jesse Owens, the champion Olympic athlete and irritator of Adolf Hitler.

Vengeance Is Sweet! Even Batman Knows That!

According to those who've seen it, other guests depicted in Murali's prize painting include former international cricket umpires Darrell Hair and Ross Emerson locked in gladiatorial combat in a pit in a nearby anteroom, while Adam 'Batman' West looks on. Hair and Emerson famously no-balled Murali for 'chucking' in the mid-1990s, before the off-spinning phenomenon's action was cleared.

Off-Spinning Record-Breaker Baffles Everybody Yet Again With Inception-Style Guest! You Won't Believe Who It Is!!

But perhaps most intriguingly of all, sources close to the doosra-wielding champion revealed that his majestic mural contains Warne himself! The leg-spinner can reportedly be seen at the back of the gathering, talking to Claude Monet, presumably about his own painting, which stands on an easel behind him.

Was Warne warned about Murali's mural? We can only imagine not. Representatives from Warne's management company declined to make the spin king available for comment on this story.

Meeting Minutes: Third Ashes Test, 2017-18

AN EXCERPT FROM 'CRICKET TEAM MANAGEMENT USING AGILE SCRUM METHODOLOGIES AND LEAN, SWIFT TECHNIQUES—2017-18 ASHES EDITION'

Modern cricket needs modern management techniques, as these minutes from England's meetings during the 2017/18 Ashes reveal.

Team Members:

Present: Joe Root, Alastair Cook, Mark Stoneman, James Vince, Dawid Malan, Jonny Bairstow, Moeen Ali, Chris Woakes, Craig Overton, Stuart Broad, Jimmy Anderson

Apologies: Ben Stokes

Quorum present? Yes

In Attendance:

Team Coach: Trevor Bayliss (non-voting)

Proceedings:

- Meeting called to order at 7:15 p.m. by Chair, Mr Root
- Minutes for Post-Third Ashes Test meeting were approved and a round of drinks ordered

Captain's Report:

- Mr Root recommended that, given that the team is no longer able to retain the Ashes, we should at least attempt to avoid a whitewash like 'those 2006-07 and '13-14 idiots'. After brief discussion (including a reminder from several of the more senior team members that previous whitewashes were to be solely blamed on Kevin Pietersen), MOTION to try to avoid whitewash was seconded and passed 10-0 (one abstain).

- Team member, Mr Cook, tabled a proposal entitled *How Not To Lose The Fourth Ashes Test*, complete with SWOT breakdown and needs analysis. Claiming he was bored, Bowling Sub-Committee Chair Mr Broad MOTIONED instead that Mr Cook just bat for three days on a dead MCG track to secure a draw. Mr Anderson seconded and the motion passed 9-1 (one abstain) Action: Mr Cook to break batting record at MCG

- Team member, Mr Bairstow, mentioned that many Barmy Army members had expressed frustration to him at having spent thousands of pounds to visit Australia for fourth and fifth Tests only to find they'd arrived to 'dead rubbers'. MOTION to ignore their plight on the grounds that it's their own silly fault for having such unrealistic expectations; seconded and passed unanimously.

Batting Sub-Committee report provided by Chair, Mr Malan:

- Mr Malan talked to the audit report from consultancy firm, PricewaterhouseCoopers (PWC), on the team's batting procedures in series so far and found them to be satisfactory, in preparation for the upcoming fourth Test. PWC confirmed that defeats in first three Tests could instead be blamed on combination of Mr Stokes' ongoing absence, the bias of the Australian media and poor performance from bowling unit. Lengthy and heated discussion ensued. MOTION to accept PWC audit of who to blame for defeat in first three Tests; seconded and passed 5-4 (two abstain). Action: Mr Cook to prepare a report on the methods of dismissal in cricket.

- Mr Malan also reviewed highlights, trends and issues from the third Test scorecard, opposition bowling figures and Barmy Army songbook. Issues include a poor ROI from Mr Ali and ongoing wickets from Nathan Lyon despite repeated Barmy Army songs about his personal life. After brief discussion of the issues and suggestions about how to ensure songs could be made more upsetting and offensive, MOTION to accept scorecards; seconded and passed 10-0 (one abstain). Action: Mr Cook to upload scorecards to team Dropbox.

Bowling Sub-Committee's report provided by Chair, Mr Broad:

- Mr Broad reminded the team of his scheduled dinner reservations at 8:30pm, and recommended everybody get on with it.

- Mr Broad offered full and unequivocal apology on behalf of the entire Bowling Sub-Committee for allowing Mitchell Marsh to score 181 in the third Test. Acknowledged this was unacceptable on any level and that the committee had no excuse. Apology was noted.

- Mr Broad presented members of the team with breakdown of Bowling Sub-Committee brainstorm session on how to dismiss Steve Smith. Final recommendation was to wait for relatively innocuous scandal to blow up in South Africa, forcing Cricket Australia to suspend their captain and best batsman for a year. After brief discussion on how stupidly implausible this was, MOTION to accept Bowling Sub-Committee recommendation on how to get Smith out was seconded; defeated 6-4 (one abstain).

- Mr Broad presented members with anecdote of how funny it was when

Ben Duckett poured a beer over Mr Anderson's head. Recommended that Duckett return to the squad immediately. MOTION to allow Duckett's return was not supported.

Other business:

- Chair proposed that given shambolic nature of Australian tour, attention should instead turn to upcoming tour of New Zealand. Chair suggested a New Zealand sub-committee be formed. Mr Cook volunteered to chair sub-committee and offered to run a kick-off workshop with key stakeholders to define the vision, goals and objectives of New Zealand tour in order to brainstorm some measurable objectives and KPIs for each stage gate. Action: Mr Cook to prepare agenda for kick-off workshop.

- Mr Bayliss announced that he had recently hired a new team masseuse. Also, a team spin bowling (off) coach, team batting (unorthodox strokes) advisor, team psychologist, team sociologist, four additional team bodyguards, team media advisor, team social media (Instagram/Snapchat) manager, team hair stylist, team feng shui consultant, team body painter, team veterinarian and team chimney sweep. Furthermore, a new team bus had been hired to carry new members of the staff, which as a result now also included a new (second) team bus driver, new team bus mechanic and new team bus systems co-ordinator. Management charts had been updated accordingly and were supplied to members.

- Meeting adjourned at 8:35 p.m.

- Minutes submitted by Secretary, Mr Cook.

'The Battles of Dawson'

AN EXCERPT FROM 'CASUALTIES OF WAUGH'

The horrors of Waugh are illustrated in gruesome detail. Here's the tale of young Richard Dawson and how Waugh scarred him for life.

Richard Dawson was 22 years old, born and bred in Doncaster, Yorkshire, and sent to the other side of the world to face the horrors of Waugh.

Richard had completed basic training eighteen months earlier in Yorkshire, and six months after that had seen minor action in Mohali, India. But none of that had prepared him for the bloodiest-minded Waugh in history.

Captain Nasser Hussain, the leader of Richard's squad, was a tough commander. A hard-nosed combatant. He'd seen more Waugh than most ordinary men could stand.

Under Hussain, England had lost many of the battles. And yet, despite those defeats, it now appeared, at long last, as if the Waugh's end might come soon.

It would. But not soon enough for poor Richard Dawson.

● ● ●

Australia had secured victory in the first four battles of the 2002/03 Ashes campaign. The margins of victory had been 384 runs, an innings and 51 runs, an innings and 48 runs, and five wickets (after enforcing the follow-on). The Australian blitzkrieg had left England a shell-shocked rabble.

But while the enemy had been routed by the might of the Australian forces, captain Steve Waugh had contributed little on the field. And there were concerns that this was a weakness the opposing forces might someday exploit against an otherwise dominant plan of attack.

The battle plan was simple but effective. Matthew Hayden and Justin Langer would blunt the enemy's attack by dropping a double century partnership on them. The residual damage from this opening onslaught would then allow a secondary wave from Ricky Ponting and Damien Martyn to move in and exploit the declining morale of the enemy. The result was inevitably carnage.

By the time Waugh arrived at the front, the battle was usually won. In the first innings of the Ashes series so far he'd come to the crease at 3/378, 3/356, 4/226 and 3/265. For a man whose career had been built on backs-to-the-wall trench warfare and stubbornly refusing to yield when confronted with an opposition force making early inroads, this was new territory to conquer. And he was struggling to do so.

Another man might have appreciated the irony that he had mustered a squad so dominant that it had undermined his own individual success. But Waugh, one senses, had little interest in the concept of irony. Did irony win cricket matches? It did not.

But now, in the fifth Test, Waugh had returned to more familiar ground. A surprise attack from the English forces had seen him summoned to action with the score at just 3/56, familiar ground to a hardened veteran who'd cut his teeth on precisely those kind of skirmishes.

It was the perfect opportunity for Waugh to recreate the dogged triumphs of his earlier campaigns. But he refused to do so. He could have dug in. He was, after all, renowned for being exactly that kind of digger. Instead, with support from the inexperienced Martin Love, Waugh boldly counter-attacked, taking his foes by surprise. He brought up a half-century in 61 balls as England were forced to regroup.

And regroup they did, striking back to take a wicket.

Alas, they would take Love, not Waugh.

But now allied with his second-in-command Adam Gilchrist, whose aerial assaults over the years had often destroyed opposing forces, Waugh set his sights on regaining the initiative and securing himself a ton.

And so with Waugh needing just five runs to bring up his century, and one over remaining in the day, Hussain brought young Richard Dawson into the front lines, tossing the ball to the young spinner.

It was a desperate ploy. And a grotesque mismatch. The wide-eyed, naïve rookie against the narrow-eyed, experienced veteran. What went through the youngster's mind as he confronted the true face of Waugh? Its horrors. Its terror. Its cold brutality.

We may never know, but reports from the front tell us that Dawson fought bravely, considering the circumstances in which he found himself. He carefully probed, forcing Waugh onto the back foot. Unfortunately for Dawson, the back foot was where his opponent was at his strongest. Waugh made the initial strike, moving to 98.

And then, the final ball. The ball that changed everything. Dawson shot it in, fast and full. Waugh picked the length early and countered with a shot of his own. The ball exploded through the covers for four. Crowd, commentators, television viewers, and batting partners all went ballistic at this grand theatre of Waugh.

●●●

Richard Dawson was 22 years old, born and bred in Doncaster, Yorkshire and sent to the other side of the world to face the horrors of Waugh.

It took just one precision shot for Richard Dawson's Test cricket career to be fatally wounded. There was no hope of recovery.

Richard Dawson was shipped back home to England, yet another casualty of Waugh.

He was just a bloody kid.

A LAMENT FOR RICHARD DAWSON

In far antipodean lands,
In cruel Australian hands
To our shame the Ashes did dwell
For three years and ten,
They'd crushed our best men
And the yearning to regain
them did swell

So we shipped him o'er the sea
Out to the SCG,
The land of Banjo and Henry Lawson
But with one blow for four
He was a casualty of Waugh,
Remember our boy, young Richard Dawson

The Art of Warner

**AN EXCERPT FROM 'ON WARNER' BY GIDEON HAIGH,
THE SEQUEL TO THE BEST-SELLING 'ON WARNE'**

The most acclaimed cricket writer in the world follows his masterful study of Shane Warne with a brilliant analysis of David Warner

In a letter to Henry L Sprague in 1900, Theodore Roosevelt wrote, "Speak softly and carry a big stick; you will go far."

It's unlikely that David Warner has studied the former American President's epistolary output in any notable depth, but perhaps, like Warner's brother Steve, who once infamously, and with great malapropism aforethought, claimed via social media that his sibling had been made an 'escapegoat' (*sic*), the gist, rather than the nitpicking minutiae, of the English language is deemed sufficient.

For Dave Warner speaks loudly, carries a big bat and has gone far. Often too far.

It is all done in the name of 'aggression', of course, the *sine qua non* of Warner's cricket. When batting, the impulse for his shot is almost always an attacking one. Warner will defend only if left with no other option; he is, it seems, a man who simply does not know the meaning of the word recreancy.

At the crease, Warner radiates hostility. For the bowler tasked with the duty of running in towards him, such an overt emanation of animus will often trigger a reciprocal escalation of ferocity.

The temptation for the garden-variety quick, whose province as aggressor in the sport's fundamental twenty-two yard *mano a mano* has been usurped by Warner's brazen bellicosity, is to pitch it short. To re-establish primacy and force Warner to back down with a targeted bouncer.

This is a mistake. A short ball to Warner invites him to pull. In the split second in which he appraises the length of the delivery, he will sway back. The manoeuvre both buys him a fraction of a second of extra time and also lowers his centre of gravity. He will then whip his puissant forearms through the trajectory of the ball—more often than not, swinging the arc up and under it.

Warner's dynamism derives, predominantly, from the power of his arms. He is supremely strong, a modern-day Herakles or Beowulf or Popeye. Between deliveries Warner will obsessively unfasten and refasten his gloves, as if to ensure his wrists remain sufficiently secured to his forearms to smite his next shot. Without exception, they are.

Invariably, the coalescence of Warner's strength and pull shot trajectory is a ball propelled to 'cow corner', an area of the ground that one suspects would, in different epochal and dialectic circumstances, be commandeered as rhyming slang for 'Dave Warner'.

A bowler in possession of a cooler head will resist the primal urge to bounce, instead pitching it up, fuller, searching for the outside edge. But even a single lapse in that investigation exposes the option for Warner to drive, most often through the covers, where his ability to find the gap is otherworldly. Again, the power with which Warner strikes the ball is such that a defeat of the infield invariably foreshadows a corresponding defeat of any outfielder in its race to the rope.

Alternatively, and more humiliatingly, Warner will drive straighter, back past the bowler who just delivered it. The vexing result is that the bowler, having kept an admirably clear mind against Warner's belligerence, is punished for that very clarity of mind.

It is impossible for an adversary to exude more hostility than Warner. The only way to defeat him is with an implementation of precise technique.

●●●

In the past 25 years we have witnessed the unambiguous evolution of the attacking Australian opening batsman. The progenitor, at least in contemporary terms, was Michael Slater, who rejected the obduracy of his immediate long-term predecessor Geoff Marsh, a man whose career is judged these days, unfairly, yet thankfully, against the standards of his sons.

Slater gave way to Matthew Hayden, a more overt manifestation of the combative approach that Slater had forged. Slater's feet gambolled down the pitch with a lightness of touch and there was a certain precision behind the scything blade. Hayden relinquished any suggestion of a lightness of touch, and he wielded not so much a blade that scythed as a battle-axe that cleaved. A man seemingly powered by the outward thrust of his chest, like some form of medieval bellows, Hayden was all brawn and bombast and brutality.

The arrival of Warner elicited a compression of Hayden's bluster, muscle and savagery into a more compact physical package. But with no corresponding diminishment of his predecessor's aggression, this merely meant a proportionate increase in its density.

Indeed, Warner may very well be the densest body of aggression Test cricket has ever seen.

The Genius of Bad Cricket

AN EXCERPT FROM 'SMART MUSINGS FOR SMART CRICKETERS' BY ED SMITH

Think deeply enough about cricket and you'll find yourself in, uh, interesting territory, as we see in these 'smart cricket' essays.

"You know I'm bad, I'm bad you know it"—Michael Jackson

"He bowls to the left, he bowls to the right, that Mitchell Johnson, his bowling is shite"—The Barmy Army

During the Vietnam war, US president Richard Nixon confided in his chief of staff, Harry Robins Haldeman, that he wanted to employ what he called the 'Madman Theory' to bring an end to the conflict. The basis of Nixon's theory was the notion that if the North Vietnamese came to believe that he was so sufficiently volatile and unpredictable that he might actually use the nuclear weapons at his disposal, then that would force them to the negotiating table.

I am reminded of Nixon's Madman Theory when I ponder future trends for cricket.

We have all seen a spinner bowl a long hop that dismisses a batsman who mistimes the ball in his eagerness to launch it out of the ground. Rarely do we consider the possibility that such a delivery might be a deliberate choice. But what if it were?

Cricket, particularly in the limited over forms of the game, exemplifies a notion that economists are familiar with: risk vs return. Shares are riskier than property which is riskier than cash. But the returns from each type of investment have the same hierarchy as the risks. To achieve higher returns, you must accept higher risks. And, conversely, decreasing one's risks requires an acceptance that you will receive correspondingly diminished returns.

Similar patterns apply in cricket. Attempting to hit a six is almost always a riskier shot than guiding a ball to third man for a single. But is it six times riskier? These are the questions that batsmen need to regularly ask themselves if they are to optimise their scores. The very best batsmen internalise these decisions, constantly modifying the point they're occupying on the risk-return frontier to match the game situation.

Bowlers play in the same risk-return areas, of course, but with the axes reversed. For example, a fast bowler can strive for a yorker that will increase the chance of dismissing a batsman but only at the risk of getting it wrong and being lofted into the stadium. The chance of an increased return (in terms of likelihood of taking a wicket) comes with the increased risk of going for runs.

And so it goes.

But how does this notion relate to the prospect of deliberately poor play? Bear with me. Because another concept worth exploring here is The Prisoner's Dilemma. Perhaps you've heard of it? The Prisoner's Dilemma is a classic game theory paradox, in which one ponders the thought process of a pair of criminal gang members, arrested but interrogated separately. Each one receives the offer of *betraying* their fellow gang member by testifying against them or *co-operating* with them by staying silent.

If a prisoner betrays their colleague by 'squealing' while their accomplice remains silent, then that prisoner will go free and their colleague will go to prison for three years. Simple enough. But the dilemma comes to light with this extra wrinkle—if they *both* choose to betray, then they both go to prison for two years. And if they both stay silent, they each go to prison for only one year.

Now imagine you're one of these prisoners—perhaps as a result of some minor literary crime. Think through your position and you'll swiftly come to the conclusion that no matter what your colleague does, you're better off betraying them. (If he—or *she*—has betrayed you, then reciprocating that betrayal reduces your sentence from three to two years. On the other hand, if your criminal colleague of indeterminate gender has kept silent, then betraying them reduces your sentence from one to zero years. Betrayal, then, is the only logical option.)

But your accomplice can apply the *exact same logic*, meaning you'll both end up betraying one another, dooming the pair of you to two years in prison. Whereas if you'd both stayed silent you'd have been out in just one year. Something has gone terribly wrong.

The Prisoner's Dilemma becomes even more interesting and relevant when we consider an *iterated* version of it. In the iterated Prisoner's Dilemma, the choice to co-operate or betray is made not just the one time, but over and over again. Now the criminals can learn from past behaviour. Now they can earn trust with one another. Now they can learn to stay silent and maximise their freedom.

Cricket can be analysed in a similar way. Batsmen and bowlers can 'betray' one another—and, as it happens, the cricket viewing public—by playing a low risk-low return game, in what is considered good, sensible cricket. Tidy bowling, conservative field placements, batsmen milking singles with no real risk of being dismissed. Nobody takes many wickets. But nobody makes many runs either. It's the very definition of 'boring middle overs' cricket.

Or somebody can move their game into a high risk-high return arena. Risky shots, attacking bowling, aggressive field placement. More runs are scored. More wickets fall. The game is more exciting. And, by the by, more *fun*.

Cricket is a simple game. For at its heart it is merely an iterated prisoner's dilemma centred around preferred risk-return quadrants.

People speak of flawed geniuses, but very few seem to reflect on the possibility that perhaps being flawed is how we *get to* genius. A risky shot—even if it leads to one's dismissal—may be just the trigger one needs to move the game into areas that, over the long term, are more profitable for you as a batsman.

Being dismissed with a 'bad' shot—say, a wild waft outside off stump—is a worthwhile sacrifice to make if it encourages bowlers to feed you future deliveries in that area from which you can profit. Eventually they'll catch on, but not before you've cashed in. Over the long term, your average will be higher than if you'd taken the conservative route and let that wide ball go.

This, then, is the modern 'Madman Theory' of cricket. Playing bad cricket is, counter-intuitively, the path to excellence in our game. And that's something that in my new role as England selector I'm very keen to explore.

'WHAT I LEARNED ABOUT MATESHIP DOWN UNDER,' BY STUART BROAD

'What I Learned About Mateship Down Under'

Editor's note: After several emails and snail mails Mr Broad filed the two preceding pages.

Bulging Lists and Unsolicited Tips

AN EXCERPT FROM 'CHILDREN'S LETTERS TO SANTNER'

What's more adorable than small children writing letters to Santa? Small children writing letters to Mitchell Santner.

LETTER ONE

Child's Letter

Dear Santner

I would like a puppy for Christmas. I promise I'd look after him properly. I'd also like a colouring book with some textas and a set of chubby Owlearmuffs.

I have been very good all year. Even to Megan when she annoys me with all her crying.

From Ella

Santner's Response

Dear Ella,

You have mistaken me for Santa Claus.
I am not Santa Claus. I am New Zealand's
premier limited overs left arm orthodox
spinner.

I'm glad you've been kind to Megan. I'm
sure Santa will bring you all the presents
you want. I'll pass your letter onto him.

Yours sincerely,

[signature]

LETTER TWO

Child's Letter

Dear Santner,

Merry Christmas. I know you are busy feeding the riendeer and making sure ~~are~~ all the elves finish their work but I want to make sure I get a playstation this year. Last year I was supposed to get one but only got a Nintendo switch. Also, do you cold up in the North Pole? I hope you have a good coat.

Love from Bobby

Santner's Response

Dear Bobby,

I am not Santa Claus. I am Mitchell Santner, a cricketer from New Zealand. While it gets cold in New Zealand sometimes, it doesn't get as cold as the North Pole. But I do have a very good coat.

I will let Santa know you specifically want a Playstation.

Yours sincerely,

LETTER THREE

Child's Letter

Dear Santner,

I have noticed that sometimes, in the death overs when the batsmen are looking to go big, you'll flatten the trajectory of your bowling arc in an attempt to avoid being hit to the boundary.

I think this is a mistake and if you were to toss the ball up, you would extract more turn from the pitch. This would enable you to catch the edge or perhaps even beat the bat entirely for a stumping. A wicket at that stage of an innings will halt the opposition momentum far more than a single or even a dot ball.

Just a thought,
   Sam.

Santner's Response

Dear Sam,

Bite me. When you're the number one ranked T20 bowler in the world with a lucrative IPL deal, maybe then you can offer me some of your simplistic advice.

Until then, mind your own damn business.

Merry Christmas,

The Perimeter of Identity

AN EXCERPT FROM 'IN SEARCH OF LOST BODILY FLUIDS, VOL. 6, RUNS 151 TO 180' BY PROFESSOR DEAN JONES

(Translated from the original,
À La Recherche De Fluides Corporels Perdus by Professeur Jones)

An epic in seven volumes, Dean Jones's book, 'À La Recherche De Fluides Corporels Perdus', tells the story of his 1986 double century in Madras. The full book is over 4,200 pages long, making it the second longest cricket book in history after Steve Waugh's autobiography, Out of My Comfort Zone.

As M Border walked towards the puddle of vomit that I had created on the left-hand side of the pitch, barely glancing at it, his attention was instead directed towards me as I heaved yet again, deepening the pool of my nauseant.

"Ugh," he said, his stern and bristle-bearded manner refusing to conceal his disdain for my illness. M. Border was an obdurate man; a laughterless customer hardened by harsh circumstances. He brooked no nonsense, and his demeanour as he stood a distance from my accumulated expectorant strongly suggested that he considered extreme dehydration and the ensuing symptoms to be a particularly brazen example of the kind of frolic he held in contempt.

"I don't think I can continue," I confessed, and in my heart I knew it to be the truth, for the relentless onslaught of the conditions had stolen all physical energy from me; and worse, my mental and spiritual energy had also been sapped in their entirety, leaving me a husk that was naught but a simulacrum of a functioning human being and cricketer.

"Yeah, well that's okay mate," said M. Border. "If you want to go off now we'll get someone tough out here. We'll get a Queenslander out here."

I was taken aback by M. Border's words. Could I be so easily replaced by M. Ritchie, a batsman I'd long considered, like most cricketers, to be an inferior?

If so, what, then, did this say about individuality? The very nature of identity? If M. Ritchie could serve the same function as me, did that not make him the same batsman as me? For if two individuals are identical in all aspects, by what manner do we distinguish them?

This was a philosophical riddle that had long plagued my mind. What *was* identity? What did it mean for something to be the same thing as itself? Where did one draw a perimeter between an individual's identity and the rest of the universe? Did such a boundary even exist?

These questions occupied my mind not just along the spatial axis, of course, but also along a chronological one. For the maintenance of an individual identity across different moments of time seemed to me to be a fundamental impossibility. By what mechanism can identity remain constant from instant to instant when there is no intermediate point by which one can make the connection necessary to maintain that identity?

As I vomited again at the side of the pitch and began to defecate in my trousers, I continued to muse on these matters.

If one's identity *is* sustainable across time, as so manifestly appears to be the case, despite the logical questions that arise from that supposition, to where does that identity depart when we die? Or, conversely, where did it exist before our birth? Does this not provide evidence that our existence is eternal, and, given that our physical bodies are so frail, as exhibited by my current state of distress in the middle of M. A. Chidambaram Stadium, surely we can safely deduce that our existence resides not in the flesh and bone of our corporeal substance but in some hitherto unmeasurable, eternal soul?

But this deduction only opens further questions for consideration. For if we are measured by a spiritual essence that has existed since the beginning of time and that will endure until the end of reality, then we must also question how that essence becomes tied to a specific embodiment. Why, for example, was I in my body, rather than M. Border's? Or M. Ritchie's? Or M. Bradman's?

Furthermore, if identity is a robust consideration that applies to all objects and concepts, both on the physical and meta-physical plane, then what do we make of the identity of non-identity? Can the concept of a lack of identity itself have an identity? And, if so, by what means? Is the only resolution to this apparent paradox to discard the notion of identity in its entirety and embrace its very opposite?

To whit, are we all different manifestations of one eternal soul, divided across not just all of humanity, but all of life and, perhaps, all of matter, thereby rendering the notion of identity moot?

I relayed the essence of these musings and my philosophical concerns to M. Border, who gave them scant heed.

"Fuck off with that shit, Deano," he said. "You're babbling with the heat. Take a single and get off strike."

I resolved to delay further philosophical considerations. Instead, I gathered myself and took fresh guard. The 179th run of my innings loomed anew in my concerns.

The Book of Botham 19:81

**AN EXCERPT FROM 'AND DID THOSE FEET IN ANCIENT TIME...
THE GOOD BOOK OF ENGLAND CRICKET'**

What possessed the International Bible Society to issue a liturgical retelling of the history of English cricket? There's only room for one cricketing bible, and Wisden's got that covered.

And there fell a final wicket, of Graham Dilley, and behold, England was all out for 174.

And Kim Hughes looked upon the first innings deficit and saw that it was good. And Hughes said, "Let there be a follow-on." And it was so.

But yea, the light did grow bad. And the overs bowled did but number three before play was stopped. But still Dennis Lillee did dismiss Graham Gooch without score. And England was 3/1 at stumps.

The odds were offered by the bookmakers and those odds were twenty-five score to one. And Lillee and Rod Marsh did espy those odds. And lo, the temptation was great, for the odds were large and peculiar.

Lillee and Marsh did then send the driver of their bus to the bookmakers' tent to place a wager for them. And Lillee did offer a tenner on England to win. And Marsh did also put forth five quid. And it was considered not remarkable, for it was a different era.

On the Sabbath Day both teams rested.

On the Fourth Day Lillee and Terry Alderman did tear through the England batsmen once more. Captains of both today and tomorrow each had their wickets struck down. Mike Brearley was dismissed for fourteen, David Gower but nine and Mike Gatting did see his pads rapped in front for a sole run.

And England was 41/4, 186 in arrears of the Australian's total of the first innings.

And so Geoff Boycott did dig in. And Peter Willey did cut with great savagery. But upon the fall of their wickets, England was 133/6. And 135/7 when Bob Taylor did cheaply fall.

Dilley did join Ian Botham at the crease. And the beefy all-rounder, did say to Dilley, "Right. Come on, let's give it some humpty."

And humpty was indeed given, in great and powerful shots. Dilley did score 56 in a partnership of five score and seventeen. And Botham scored with even greater haste, as he did humpty from 39 at tea to a century soon after.

With great and reckless abandon were boundaries struck. And one six was struck from the bowling of Alderman into a stall of confectionery. And the shot was sweet.

And England did take the lead.

And when Dilley did fall, Botham did continue to humpty.

Chris Old was the new partner for Botham. And Botham said unto him, "Be strong and courageous. Be not afraid or terrified because of them, for Beefy, your all-rounder goes with you; he will never leave you nor forsake you." And Old did make 29 in a partnership of 67.

And England's lead did near one hundred.

And when Old did fall, Botham looked upon the batting prowess of Bob Willis and chose to humpty still more.

And Willis was shielded from the strike. And Botham did humpty. And at stumps, England's lead was 124.

On the Fifth Day, Willis fell early to the bowling of Alderman. And England's final lead was 129.

Australia did commence its chase, and Botham took the wicket of Graeme Wood for ten. But the batting of Trevor Chappell and the batting of John Dyson was robust and as lunch did near, the score was 56/1.

And so Brearley did switch the end of Willis, for he did covet a breakthrough. And Willis now bowled down the hill and with the wind. And Brearley did advise Willis to not worry about no-balls. And he did say unto him, "Just run up and bowl fast and straight and true."

And Willis did bowl fast. And Willis did bowl straight. And Willis did bowl true. And the change did bring immediate dividends, as Willis bounced out Chappell.

Hughes then came to the crease. But he did not make a run as Willis took his wicket also.

And two balls hence, Graham Yallop was also caught from the bowling of Willis. And Yallop also did not trouble the scorers.

And at lunch, Australia was 58/4.

After both teams had taken their fill of sandwiches and cakes and tea, the leg stump of Allan Border was removed by Old. And he, also, had made no runs.

And then when Willis did once more bowl short and Dyson did edge behind, Australia was 68/6. And in the stands, the faithful were singing hymns of joy.

The compulsion of Marsh to hook was known throughout all the lands, and Willis did now feed this unquenchable desire. And the outfield catch was taken and Australia was 74/7.

Geoff Lawson then also did fall to the venom of Willis. And Australia was 75/8.

And Hughes cried out in a loud voice, "My team, my team, why have you forsaken me?"

Kim Hughes wept.

Now consider the Lillee on the field, how his innings grows. He toils hard, with Ray Bright, who does not spin. And the pair did put on 35 for the ninth wicket.

But Lillee was caught by Gatting, and Bright did succumb to a yorker. And Willis did finish with figures of 8/43.

Cricket so loved the world that it gave its one and only miracle: the resurrection at Headingley. England had won by eighteen runs.

'Author' biographies

Approvals for the content in this book would have come from the publishers had they existed.

Dan Liebke, the creator of *The Instant Cricket Library,* is grateful to those whose contributions to the game of cricket inspired this imagined anthology. The imagined authors are:

Lady Jessie Bradman was the wife of Sir Donald Bradman and also the leading authority on which batsmen most resembled him.

Shane Warne is a poker player and former star of *I'm A Celebrity Get Me Out Of Here.* He is also the greatest leg-spinner of all time.

Sir Arthur Conan Morris was a best-selling author of the popular Sherlock Hohns mysteries and a formerly dependable opening batsman for his country.

Kevin Pietersen is a South African-born English Test cricketer known for his inventive stroke play and his prodigious autobiographical musings.

The Douglas Jardine Estate is responsible for maintaining the standards and ethos of former England captain and Bodyline progenitor Douglas Jardine.

Enid Blyton was a world-famous children's author who specialised in tales of such enumerated groups as the Famous Five and the Secret Seven but never, alas, an Electrifying Eleven.

Henry Blofeld is a once dashing commentator for the BBC whose musings while on air have sometimes been known to mention the cricket.

George R.R. Bailey is an Australian cricketer and acclaimed fantasy author whose epic series and backwards batting stance have both crossed into mainstream culture.

Andy Bichel is one of Australia's finest ever 12th men who, to his eternal dismay, was a key member of the undefeated 2003 World Cup playing eleven.

Shane Watson is an accomplished all-rounder, an Allan Border medallist, the 44th Test captain of Australia and occasional LBW candidate.

J.L.R. Previtera aka 'Joe the Cameraman' is widely agreed to be the greatest ever cricket-writing cameraman and analyst of bowling and throwing.

Tim Miller is an expert on ICC Associate cricket and a tireless, yet exhausting, advocate for the expansion of the number of teams eligible for full international status.

Ed Cowan is a former Test opening batsman considered, in certain cricket and non-cricket circles, to be one of Australia's most refined, intelligent and thoughtful cricketers.

Mark Nicholas is a former first-class cricketer and now cricket commentator whose smooth tones, and English accent were welcomed into Australia with as open arms, as one could reasonably expect.

Ellyse Perry is a champion all-rounder for the Australia's women's cricket team. In her spare time she also displays peerless excellence in a variety of other pursuits.

'Author' biographies

Paul 'Frogless' Adams is a South African leg-spinner and science fiction author whose books are widely considered to be almost as funny as his bowling action.

Damien Fleming is a former Australian swing bowler and one of the most fearsome wielder of metaphors in modern cricket commentary.

Neil Harvey is a member of Australia's 1948 undefeated 'Invincibles' Ashes team, but most famous today for his forthright comparisons of contemporary and departed cricketers.

Mike Hussey is a movie critic and former Australian Test batsman whose boundless enthusiasm earned him the nickname Mr Cricket and, less commonly, Mr Cinema.

Brendon McCullum is a former New Zealand captain renowned just as much for his sense of decency and fair play as his aggressive batting and leadership.

Jarrod Kimber used to blog about cricket.

Neville Cardus was a celebrated cricket writer and as beloved a figure in the history of the English game as W. G. Grace, county cricket and tedious rain delays.

Matthew Hayden is a former Australian opening batsman, fisherman and BBQ-er whose award-winning novellas encapsulate all facets of his personality.

Gideon Haigh is one of the finest cricket writers in the universe and sensibly forsook the opportunity to write a foreword to this anthology.

Ed Smith is a cricket writer and thinker on the game whose intellectual musings opened the door for him to become England's cleverest ever national selector.

Stuart Broad is an England fast bowler renowned for the length of his run up, his reluctance to walk, and his rare capacity to enrage Australian cricket followers.

Mitchell Santner is a New Zealand spin-bowling all-rounder who is occasionally mistaken for Santa Claus.

Professor Dean Jones is a former Australian batsman whose epic double century in India was the cornerstone of a tied Test and topic for an equally epic, multi-volume novel.

The author continues his search for the lost and forgotten literary output of cricket's greats. Correspondence and intelligence can be passed on via Twitter @LiebCricket

Real Author Biography

Dan Liebke is a comedy writer and former Nathan Hauritz impersonator. He was a regular contributor for *MAD* magazine in Australia for two decades before coming to his senses and turning his comic focus to cricket.

In addition to a social media presence on Twitter (@liebcricket), Dan has also contributed articles making fun of cricket and cricketers to websites such as *The Guardian, Cricket365* and *FirstPost*. He's also a regular on the *Can't Bowl, Can't Throw* cricket podcast and *White Line Wireless* internet radio commentary.

Liebke was once the official scorer for ABC Radio for a Test, which was rather a neat trick as it was the first time he'd ever scored a cricket match. (Shhh, don't tell Aunty). Dan is a genuine all-rounder, equally inept with both bat and ball, and he steadfastly believes that cricket is the funniest, and hence best, sport that humanity has ever invented.

AUTOGRAPHS